Silent in the Shroud

a seventh-century inscription
from Wales

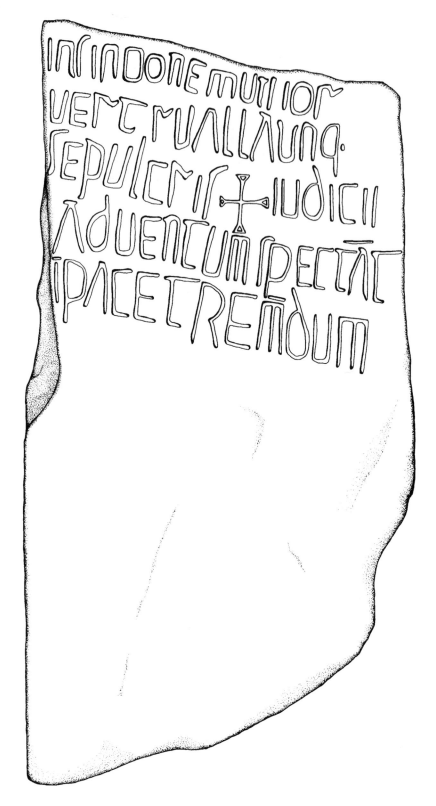

Frontispiece   *The slab, with its inscription*
(drawn from a mosaic of detailed photographs by Carl Thorpe, 1994)

Silent in the Shroud

a seventh-century inscription
from Wales

CHARLES THOMAS

The Pinkfoot Press
Balgavies, Angus
1999

First published in Scotland in 1999 by
The Pinkfoot Press
Balgavies, Forfar, Angus DD8 2TH

ISBN 1 874012 21 0

Typographic realisation by David Henry
Produced and designed at The Pinkfoot Press

Printed by Burns Harris and Findlay Ltd, Dundee

Contents

Illustrations

Foreword

Llanlleonfel (Llanllywenfel) is, or can be, on the road from the Severn Bridge to Lampeter. On my many visits to the former St David's University College (1828), now University of Wales Lampeter where I am fortunate to hold a honorary Fellowship, I find myself driving north across the Beacons, the upper Usk basin and the Epynt plateau before turning west to Llandovery. A brief sojourn at Llanllywenfel church invariably detains me – I have lost count of how many times in the last decade – and on each occasion some new aspect of the seventh-century inscription here called prosaically *986 Ioruert* has been the reward. It was a darkening January afternoon when, staring at the great stone, I noticed that the adjacent lectern Bible was open at St Matthew's Gospel, Chapter 10. Idly converting the Good News English back into the Latin of the Vulgate, in a flash I saw that the names of the twelve Disciples were also the twelve words on the stone. (The late M.R. James would have made much of this incident.) Analytical study of this particular inscription is only a small part of a wider programme, one that has led to several published reports and now (1998) a first descriptive handbook, *Christian Celts: Messages and Images* (Tempus, Stroud). Within that, *986 Ioruert* is included (chap.7) but only very briefly, and before I found its Old Testament aspect, because it is just one of many remarkable Biblical-style compositions from post-Roman western and northern Britain. It may, however, be ranked among two or three crowning achievements by Christian authors whose names can now be revealed. I would not dare assert that, since 1996, I have perceived and de-coded all its allusions, devices, messages and pictures; but there cannot be much left to find, and what has so far been found surely merits (as here) speedy publication in its own right.

I am grateful to Ellis Evans for expert detailed comment on the personal names; Mark Redknap, National Museum of Wales, for various most useful archive details; Reverend Jonathan Smith, Rector of Llangammarch Wells, who so kindly undertook local enquiries for me; Carl Thorpe for several of the new illustrations; and above all to David Howlett, discoverer and exponent of Biblical-style compositions within Insular writings, for unceasing help and inspiration since I first began to explore this parallel world of writings on stone. So many of his own insights appear here that I cannot always disentangle them from my own, but (as he would agree) the true reward of such shared excitement is to reach a stage where this hardly matters. Last, but only in order of mention, it is a pleasure to be associated with the Pinkfoot Press and David Henry, an enthusiast and a publisher of vision to whom a large world of Celtic studies is greatly indebted; and he and I would record our special thanks to a religious Trust, at its own request un-named, for a generous subvention towards cost.

The Setting

LLANLLEONFEL (its map name) or Llanllywenfel, the older version, is a small Victorian church with a graveyard in the county of Brecon at NGR SN 938499. Its patron saint is lost. Recently a 'Saint Onfel' seems to have been invented by folk-etymology (*lle* 'place' of-Onfel).[1] It is not known what the place name really means and the necessary early forms of it are missing. The church is on a wooded hillock up to which a lane, microscopically signposted, leads south off the A483, Builth-Wells to Llandovery road west of Garth village. It is sub-parochial, a chapelry to Llangammarch Wells, which is rectorial over Llanganten and Llanfechan (Llanafanfechan) also. In previous centuries Llanllywenfel was the only perpetual curacy without tithes or parsonage-house under the prebendary of Llanwrthwl. Even its name is variable. In this neighbourhood, still noticeably bilingual, I have collected three further oral forms of which 'Llanllywel' is perhaps the favourite.

The notional parish has 1508 acres. It may have started as an ancient holding within the manor held by the Gwynnes of Garth until their disappearance in the early 19th century. In the eighteenth, the church was well maintained, almost as the Gwynne family chapel; John Wesley, A.M., officiated here in 1749 at the wedding of his brother Charles to Sarah Gwynne. By 1873 'poor old Llanleonfel church [was] now in ruins' when the diarist Francis Kilvert attending the Garth Flower Show, Dog Show, Poultry Show, Bazaar and Athletic Sports (all in one) strolled up to it, and disturbed several 'white owls' in the process.[2] Soon afterwards the church was rebuilt and there is a slight, sloping, rubble-spread under the grass, east and north. Today it serves a small Church in Wales congregation (first and third Sundays). Within, fixed upright, is an inscribed stone whose nature more than repays any number of visits to this lonely and peaceful spot, more often attended by sheep than by humans.

In 1699 the stone was reported as standing 'on end in Lhan Lhywenvel churchyard at the east end'.[3] An account of 1920[4] claims that 'a highly interesting stone was discovered in Llanlleonfel churchyard in 1904', most probably its re-discovery among encroaching shrubs and weeds, and in 1905 casts of it were made for the National Museum of Wales. It was still outside in 1924,[5] and in the 1930s when V.E. Nash-Williams, on fieldwork for his subsequent *The Early Christian*

Monuments of Wales (Cardiff 1950; here, ECMW), saw it. Around 1945 when R.A.S. Macalister, similarly engaged for vol.ii of his *Corpus Inscriptionum Insularum Celticarum* (Dublin, i, 1945; ii, 1949; here, CIIC), came to the place he recorded that 'since then (1924) it has been moved into the church'. Unhappily both the site and the stone escaped notice by J.O. Westwood (compiler of the earlier *Lapidarium Walliae: The Early Inscribed and Sculptured Stones of Wales*, Oxford 1876–79), a great pity because Westwood's usual detailed description would have filled gaps in the record. Recent (1998) enquiry in the neighbourhood[6] allows a conclusion that the stone was probably moved into the church in 1938–1939, but that no record was kept and that there are no surviving witnesses to the event.

The slab is now clamped upright under a window by the east end of the south inner wall of the nave. Of local rock, a dense sandstone or gritstone, the upper part of its face shows five lines of lettering (*Frontispiece*). For the benefit of the (few) visitors the letters are usually chalked-in and a framed translation hangs on the wall. The thicker (right) edge has two, less obvious, small equal-armed crosses with barred terminals (see Fig.8). On the other face, hard to see and harder still to photograph, low down are two shallowly pocked ring crosses, like hot-cross buns, with traces of an incomplete third one (Fig.12).

The inscription is complete and (in my view) fully legible, though a few letters (underdotted, below) have been slightly damaged. There are five lines, mostly bookhand (half-uncial) letters, with a few closer to capitals; no word separation, spaces defining words; a small cross in the middle line; and four marks of abbreviation, a dot and three small bars. In the transcript, using capitals, / marks ends of lines, and letters omitted by abbreviation are supplied in lower case, bracketed. What can be read is this:

IN SINDONE MUTI IOR/UERT RUALLAUNQ.(ue) / SEPULCRIS +

IUDICII / ADUENTUM SPECTĀ(n)T / Ī(n) PACE TREM̄(en)DUM.

It means: 'Silent in the shroud, Ioruert and Ruallaun, in the graves + await in peace the dreadful coming of the judgement'. There are 12 words; as shown, 72 letters; and as read aloud slowly, 30 syllables.

We have a memorial to two men whose names, found elsewhere in early Wales,[7] mark them as Britons; Christians, because of the cross and the wording. No other information is given. Readers who know the New Testament in Latin, the *editio vulgata* or Vulgate version by St Jerome and his circle that reached Britain some time after the 420s, or who know the Gospels well, will realise that the rare word **SINDON** 'fine cotton; shroud or winding-cloth of the same', here unique among Insular inscriptions, occurs in the Gospels in the context of Christ's burial.[8] (The object itself is claimed by some to have survived as the Turin Shroud.[9]) Some readers, then and now, might also notice that eleven of the 13 letters of **IN SINDONE MUTI** are repeated in the Vulgate, Matthew 27.59 – IN*volvit illud* SINDONE MU*nda* 'he wrapped it [the body] in a clean winding-cloth'.

The slab, housed in its remote little church, is interesting, but not outstandingly impressive. There are a hundred and more stones, some not dissimilar, to be seen throughout Wales and in Cornwall. Yet *986 Ioruert* (as this may be called[10]) is not just another stone. It is a veritable Treasure of Wales. This paper explains why.

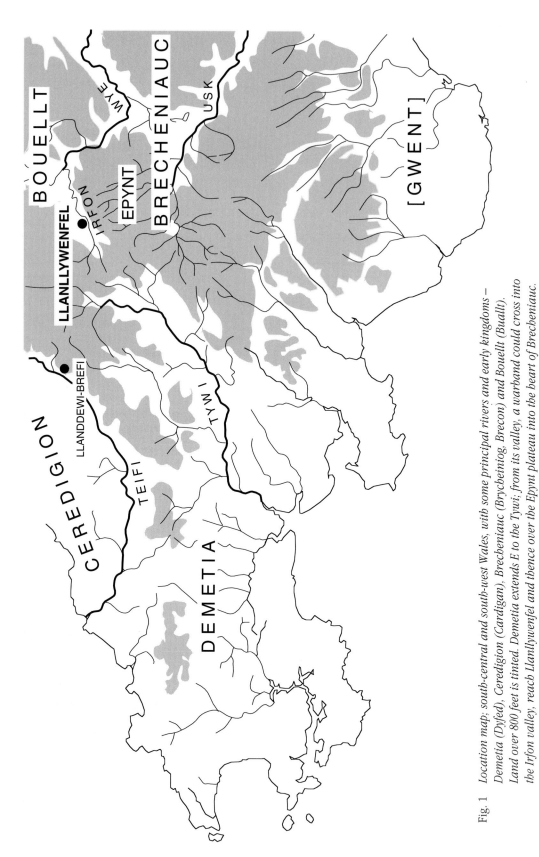

Fig. 1 *Location map: south-central and south-west Wales, with some principal rivers and early kingdoms –
Demetia (Dyfed), Ceredigion (Cardigan), Brecheniauc (Brycheiniog, Brecon) and Bouellt (Buallt).
Land over 800 feet is tinted. Demetia extends E to the Tywi; from its valley, a warband could cross into
the Irfon valley, reach Llanllywenfel and thence over the Epynt plateau into the heart of Brecheniauc.*

Historical Identifications

Several hundred proper names, predominately of men, occur in these inscriptions. Some perpetuate Roman names (Severus, Iustus), a few are Irish (Ulcagnas, Quenatauci) but most are British; Old Welsh or Old Cornish. A much larger collection of names, also for the most part British, is preserved in genealogies, annals, witness-lists to charters and minor historical sources. Ideally enough people memorialised on stone in the first list should be identifiable in the greater second list to provide a framework of approximate or absolute dates for inscriptional features. In practice the overlap is disappointingly minimal. Nash-Williams listed a dozen such identifications[11] which he dated from c.530 to c.1150. Six at least would not now be accepted, nor in any case would be some of his proposed dates.[12]

With the two names in *986 Ioruert* a starting point is the apparent fact that persons so commemorated do not represent the whole spectrum of contemporary society. Memorials are heavily weighted towards kings and princes, prominent churchmen, what can be described as aristocrats, and heads of land-holding families.[13] Elaborate inscriptions in Biblical style point at once to important people, not the peasantry. The identifications proposed here gain some credence from this, even if they cannot be claimed as anything better than historical models that do not conflict with inferences arising from the text of the inscription.

Llanllywenfel is in broken country, low hills and valleys with tributaries to the river Irfon, below the northern scarp of the (Mynydd) Epynt plateau (map, Fig.1). Epynt itself probably formed an unexploited upland within the kingdom of Brecheniauc, Brycheiniog, crossed by the ancient route, now the lonely B4591 Upper Chapel road, that explains the name (*epo-sento* 'horse-path'). North-east of Epynt lay a smaller kingdom or territory, its post-Roman name (*bou-ellt* 'cattle pasture-land') preserved by Builth (Wells), in Welsh Buallt. West from Llanllywenfel and Garth, the present road down to Llandovery and the broad vale of the river Towy (Tywi; Ystrad Tywi) follows, after Beulah Village and Llanwrtyd, the general course of a Roman road.[14] What goes one way, goes another; the route is one by way of which an attack on Brycheiniog, across Epynt, could be mounted from the Towy valley and beyond.

Until its 6th-century renaming as *Brecheniauc*, Brycheiniog, after the Christian king Brachan,[15] this kingdom – as a smaller *territorium*, the upper Usk, the corridor north to the Wye and some surrounding mountainsides – was perhaps called *Garth madrun* '(land of) the mountain-spur of Matrona'. Unusually, a sequence of names of rulers covering some three centuries can be pieced together from a number of later records. It is a regnal succession list rather than an unbroken genealogy though doubtless there are father-to-son parts in it. Our concern must be first with this sequence from Oxford, Bodleian Library, Jesus College MS20:[16]

> Ruallawn m[ap] [= 'son'] Idwallawn m. Llowarch m. Rigeneu m. Rein dremrud m. Brachan

in which the spelling might be described as Middle Welsh, though the parent collection of genealogies could be a 10th-century compilation. Brachan, his second son and successor Rein, and Rein's son Rigeneu are figures of the 6th century; that would place the next three within the 7th. By collating the above with other 'pedigrees', notably for Demetia, Dyfed, the rather larger kingdom (Pembroke, much of Carmarthen) to Brycheiniog's west, it is apparent that a Brycheiniog sequence ends with Ruallawn, above. His daughter Keindrech, 'Fair-of-face', *Keindrec merch Ruallawn* in JC 20, was wed to Caden, son of the king of Dyfed. London, British Library, Harleian MS 3859,[17] identifies him as Cathen map Cloten. After this, Dyfed and Brycheiniog successions are one and the same for the next three generations.

On various grounds it can be deduced that the union may have been, politically, lopsided and that after Ruallawn the kingdom of Brycheiniog became in some fashion subservient to Dyfed. It continued as a geographical entity until the Norman lordship of Brecon, but its occasionally-named rulers may have been subordinates, *reguli*, 'petty kings'. Trying to date such dynastic happenings by ready-reckoning, counting 30 or 25 years to generations that may really be shorter reigns, is notoriously unreliable. But in order to accommodate annalistic dates for deaths of kings of Dyfed in the 8th and 9th centuries[18] the union of Keindrech and Cathen has to be assigned to the 7th, perhaps better mid-7th, *c.*640–670.

Were this king Ruallawn to be identified with the inscription's **RUALLAUN**, where does that leave the **IORUERT**, who does not figure in these JC 20 and Harl. 3859 lists? It seems an eminently reasonable guess that the real Ioruert(h) was Ruallawn's son, that both fell together (as the memorial must show) and that the daughter Keindrech was left as a dynastic heiress. The further guess, for this model, would be that the occasion was a battle on Brycheiniog's North border – the relatively insignificant *Bouellt*, Buallt, may have been only dependent territory, as it was again much later[19] – and that the enemy on this occasion was Dyfed. Marriage of the defeated ruler's daughter to the victor's son, the vanquished kingdom as a species of dowry, may have been the price exacted for a defeat.

If this is what actually happened, many of the conclusions to be drawn from the wording and the deeper interpretations of the inscribed text fall into place and make good sense together. There is an additional colour to this. It follows from two or more assumptions, neither in the least improbable. The first is that, even if the inscription's date cannot be more closely refined than the seventh century, there is every indication that it considerably post-dates 540, the year in (or close to) which Gildas's tract *De Excidio Britonum* was made public, and that the author of *986 Ioruert* was like many Insular writers[20] familiar with DEB. The second is that in the postulated 640–670 period it was within memory or record in Brycheiniog that the kingdom's plight had happened before. Probably at the end of the 5th century a king Teuderic, having no son but a daughter Marchel, was obliged to obtain for her a husband (Anlach, the father of Brachan) from the royal kin-group of Dyfed.[21]

In his Preface to DEB Gildas develops with great skill the topos that the British race, during the 4th and 5th centuries, was constantly punished by God for a series of moral shortcomings and departures from the true light of the Faith in much the same way that Jehovah punished the Children of Israel, described piecemeal in the first five books of the Old Testament (the Pentateuch) that end with Moses's death and the Israelites under Joshua about to enter the Promised Land. All such shortcomings are specified. All major reverses are attributed to Divine sorrow and anger. We can have no idea what alleged backsliding and wrongdoing anybody may have chosen to detect in Brycheiniog before the death of Ruallaun, but the tenor of the subsequent (Old Testament) interpretation of the inscription's inner text strongly implies that its composer took his cue from Gildas.[22] If the author perceived any element of, typically Biblical, repetition in the historical circumstances of Teuderic (a pagan?) having to marry his daughter Marchel (one supposes, a Christian[23]) to a Dyfed princeling, and now the rather similar union of Keindrech to Cathen of Dyfed, that too could have implied God's stern hand intervening in the affairs of Brycheiniog. Beyond this, reconstruction can degenerate into mere speculation. The interpretations offered here, in particular the Old Testament parallels, none the less appear to support these observations.

9

Literary Aspects of the Inscriptions

With rare exceptions[24] the inscriptions on stone in western and northern Britain, 5th to 11th centuries, are in Latin. Past assertions that certain inscriptions show barbarisms, provincialisms, mis-spellings, errors from ignorance and a progressive breakdown of grammar and the use of cases are almost entirely wrong. They arise from failures to understand that every word, letter and spelling is intentional and that inner meanings (hitherto both unsuspected and unperceived) dictated the visible displays. The Latin represents the standard literary Late or post-classical language and those who composed in it had for the most part fully mastered it through prolonged training in what was virtually a second tongue.

986 Ioruert offers itself first as a face-value literary composition. As David Howlett has shown,[25] it is Latin verse, a hexametric couplet scanned as below (word, syllable and letter totals).

	W	S	L
In sindone muti Ioruert Ruallaunque sepulcris	6	14	40
+ iudicii adventum spectant in pace tremendum	6	14	38 (39)

There is one false quantity, in *muti* (long –u–); the first –u– in *Ruallaunque*, as an unstressed 'w' sound, is lost by synizesis;[26] the final (long) –i– in *iudicii* is lost by elision with *a(duentum)*. On paper the syllable count is reduced from 30 to 28 (triangular; p.18). Allowing the cross (+), in line 2, to count as a 'letter' the three totals show near-complete bipartition; halves, in mean ratio (p.18). Though they need not be shown, there are the customary internal rhymes and alliterations. The necessary demonstration is that the text, whatever it may prove to hold, can be arranged as two lines of dactylic hexameter verse and in that respect is to be placed squarely within the enormous body of Insular Latin metrical writing from this period.

Chiasmus (Greek, 'a crossing'), adjective chiastic, is a long established literary figure comprising a statement followed by its re-statement in reversed or inverted order; the Vulgate offers many intricate examples.[27] Inscriptional chiasmus, where so few words are available, takes a specialised shape in which paired elements or terms are matched not so much by meaning as by being the same parts of speech and having letters in common. Something at least of this development may have arisen from imitation of the Vulgate (p.41). We can detect here a three-fold chiasmus:

a	**IN SINDONE MUTI**	3 words; In + noun abl.; adjective	N D E M U
b	**IORUERT RUALLAUNQUE**	2 words; subject for b'	U (as /u/) E T U A N
c	**SEPULCRIS**	1 word; present predicament	U C I
c'	**IUDICII**	1 word; future predicament	U C I (or I U C)
b'	**ADUENTUM SPECTANT**	2 words; verb for b	U (as /u/) E T U A N
a'	**IN PACE TREMENDUM**	3 words; In + noun abl.; adjective	E N D U M

Most of the 25 or so Insular inscriptions in Biblical style appear to be chiastic; even a text as short as the 7th-century Anglesey slab, *970 Catamanus,* with only eight words.[28] It requires some practice to detect an inscriptional chiasmus because, as above, terms are paired in a combination of ways (length, sense, parts of speech, common letters) that may seem clumsy alongside, say, Jerome's long and elegant chiastic passages but none the less produce this literary ornament.

The text can also be quartered; that is, presented as four segments each with three words. Letter totals are as shown:

1	**IN SINDONE MUTI**	13
2	**IORUERT RUALLAUNQUE SEPULCRIS**	27
3	**IUDICII ADUENTUM SPECTANT**	23
4	**IN PACE TREMENDUM**	15
		78

The intentional nature of the quartering is then confirmed by its chiastic nature:

	Syllables	First Letter	Letter U
1	6	**I** as vowel /i/	**U** as vowel /u/
2	9	**I** as /i̯/ ('y')	**U** as /u̯/ ('w') . /u/ . /u/ (3)
3	9	**I** as /i/	/u/ . **U** as /u̯/ . /u/ (3)
4	6	**I** as /i/	**U** as /u/

– with an obvious ab/b'a' pattern. The purpose was, however, to isolate six words of the twelve. There are quite a few triangular numbers shown; quarter 4 has 15 letters ($\Delta5$; see p.18), 1 and 4 have 28 ($\Delta7$), initials I_9 I_9 I_9 I_9 make 36 ($\Delta8$) and last letters I_9 S_{17} T_{18} M_{11} make 55 ($\Delta10$). (See p.17 for an explanation of these values attached to letters.) It is '36' that is repeated because quarters 1 (13 letters) and 3 (23) also produce it. With hindsight (and by the end of this paper) we can see the importance of the demonstration; the more so because, among these triangulars, 36 alone is also a square, and of the first key number, six. Of the quarters as words, semantic units, three 'sub sentences' using the only verb are possible; **IN SINDONE MUTI IUDICII ADUENTUM SPECTANT, IORUERT RUALLAUNQUE SEPULCRIS IUDICII ADUENTUM SPECTANT** and **IUDICII ADUENTUM SPECTANT IN PACE TREMENDUM**. Letter totals are 36, 50 and 38. Only 36 is both triangular and square. Neither 50 nor 38 is either. There will be other ways in which essential redeployment of these particular 36 letters is signalled but this, the first, comes from the inscription as a literary creation rather than from its mathematical computus.

Language, Epigraphy and Previous Comments

Nash-Williams's (only?) inspection of the stone at Llanllywenfel will have been in the 1930s when its location was still 'Churchyard'. He would also have been able to examine the National Museum of Wales 1905 cast (no.06.507). A drawing of the inscription, ECMW fig.51, made for him from a photograph, ECMW pl.xxi, suggests that either in 1905 or at the time of the visit the upper left corner, which is slightly damaged, may have been further obscured by lichen or moss. The ECMW transcript as [Ī (n) S] IN [D]ONE MUT I IOR for line 1 implies, wrongly, that the -N of the opening 'IN' was omitted and a suspension-mark (bar) cut over the I. Close inspection does not bear this out.

Nash-Williams noted that the text 'is an example of a metrical epitaph', and that the phrase *In sindone* 'occurs in the Book of Kells'.[29] More interestingly, he could report that the formula *Iudicii adventum tremendum* 'is of fairly common occurrence on 5th and 6th-century tombstones in Italy'.[30] It is not, as far as I can ascertain, from the Vulgate; there can be no implication that the Llanlleonfel author imitated epitaphs at such a remove, and a likely explanation is of a common source in some commentary or patristic work that was known in Britain. For the lettering, Nash-Williams observed 'Roman capitals (A, C, E, L, P, R)' mixed with half-uncials as the majority of letter-forms; this led him to assign the inscription to (his Group II) '7th–9th century'.

Within that extreme bracket, AD 600 to 900, the two (male) names may be described as Old Welsh, or Archaic Old Welsh, and the manner of spelling them within the Roman 20-letter ABC as Neo-Brittonic. **IORUERT** comprises *ior-*, Middle Welsh *ïor*, loosely translated 'lord', and *-uerth*, now *gwerth* 'worth, value'. After 600 it might have been, but was not, written IORUERTH, the two-letter or digraph -TH (as in our 'bath, moth') having probably spread to Wales from Ireland about this time. **RUALLAUN** one would have expected to find written as RIUALLAUN. The first element is *ri-* 'king', from the British *rix* (nom.), *rigos* (gen.); the second, an adjective, *uellān-os*, meaning uncertain but presumably in the area of 'famous, valorous'. Had this name appeared on a stone in the late 5th or the 6th century, attempts to represent a changing sound of the last vowel might have given *RIUALLON. In due course the lengthened open o, from the earlier long a (*uellān-*), became written with -au particularly in final syllables. When this began is open to debate. Kenneth Jackson in 1953 was reluctant to place it before the 8th century;[31] with that belief, he managed to get Nash-Williams to agree that 'a date in the eighth century is perfectly feasible for this' (with some very unconvincing reasons for writing so.[32]) Jackson, also for linguistic reasons, corrected the inscribed name to **R(I)UALLAUN** ('probably eighth century') uncharacteristically, and also unjustifiably. There is not the slightest trace of the inserted **I**, nor was it ever intended.

R.A.S. Macalister may have visited Llanllywenfel around 1945, by which time (as he commented) the stone was within the church.[33] Unable apparently to make out the left-hand part of line 1, he suggested a reading of **TUMULO LAPIDIS**? ('In a tomb of stone'), though his own illustration (plate LI) is closer to **IN SINDONE** and he, subsequently inspecting the 1905 cast at Cardiff, 'was obliged to admit... that this reading [**SINDONE MUTI**] could not be ruled out altogether, though the stone itself never suggested it to me'.

These comments, from established scholars of great experience and authority, were then (and remain) valid to some extent; unless one now chooses to think, as many do, that letter forms and especially the proportion of capitals to half-uncials (or vice-versa) give very little guide to date, and that the spelling (r(i)uall)AUN is perfectly possible before 700 – just as may be that of Ruallaun's kingdom, *Brecheniauc*, (*Brochanioc*?) 'Brycheiniog'.

More radical and far more controversial would be the opinion that the actual **IORUERT** and **RUALLAUN** on the stone are spellings chosen for non-linguistic reasons; that, if **IUDICII ADUENTUM TREMENDUM** was borrowed (if so, it was the cornerstone of the text), it has to be divided by **SPECTANT IN PACE**; and that an opening **I(n)** – with no 'N' cut – is immediately ruled out by the computus. The further contention of this opinion would be that an inscription composed in Biblical style is to a large degree guaranteed (its text is 'fixed') against any partial loss; were every third letter in line 1 deliberately chiselled out, **IN .IN.ON. MU.I I.R /**, the line could be reconstituted for half-a-dozen reasons.

What then can be said about the lettering? What are the epigraphic considerations and do they suggest any particular date? In all discussion on these Insular writings on stone there has long been, and there still is, far too much loose thinking about the respective roles of the *ordinator* (author or composer of a text) and the *lapidarius* (who actually cut the inscription). In ancient Rome and the other Imperial foci of high civilisation, where monuments for the dead were ordered at specialist shops, no doubt many stonemasons employed *ordinatores* able to provide stock or custom-made epitaphs. In post-Roman Wales that would be less likely, and not likely at all in the case of some incredibly complex Biblical-style memorials. Here it is quite

Fig. 2   *Lettering on the inscription. The author's hand, as reproduced (modified) by the cutter. Letters A, an 'open A', and the last R, are really capitals; the D is more like an uncial form; all the rest, despite vertical exaggeration and the cutter's 'squaring-off', could be called Insular half-uncials, the N, first two Rs, long S and T being acceptable forms of this.*

inconceivable (as will be shown later) that our author personally cut the letters. If he came to Llanllywenfel burial-ground himself, it would have been to officiate at the burial of Ruallaun and Ioruert, to advise on the form of their tomb and to implore prayers for their souls. The memorial would begin as an idea, the connected messages that he wished to convey, the pictorial images that would crown the work; then the wording would have been planned on slate or wax tablets or whatever served him as a note-pad; finally, on some disposable object (none has ever been found archaeologically) he would most carefully scratch out the precise pattern, line by line, letter by letter, that he wished to see reproduced. That would be handed to a stonemason or cutter whose sole task was to reproduce it, with equal care. The author would not expect to hang around Llanllywenfel for a day, or two days, carving the 'lightly and neatly picked' (so ECMW) letters on the slab.

His pattern used 15 of the available 20 letters. They were A C D E I L M N O P Q R S T U (see Fig.2). In abbreviating his final, mental, model with 78 letters to a display with 72, he used

15

two abbreviating-symbols; a dot after **Q**, for **Q(ue)**, and small bars above the line to mark omitted **N**s in **I(n)**, **SPECTA(n)T** and (last line) **TREM(en)DUM**. This is manuscript usage.[34] The letters may look slightly unusual, because most are unduly heightened, made tall and thin. Because the cutter apparently found vertical strokes the easier (and was probably more at home with capitals) there is a tendency to 'square off' letters **C E M N U**. But what we have (at one remove) is very personal; this is the author's own hand, his 'lower case' bookhand, used by him in everyday writing. It is idiosyncratic because he preferred a sort of 'open **A**', like **V** upside-down with a little top piece, and a **T** with similar small lower-hook. Strictly, it is a mixed hand; most letters are normal half-uncial, two closer to capitals. One strong clue may exist in line 5, where the **R** in **TREMDUM** differs from all the preceding **R**s. It could be argued (anticipating the explanation of the computus that follows) that the sequence **I P A C E T *R* E M D U M** contains: a run of (key number) six letters, a distinctive '**R**', value 16 (or square of four), and a run of (key number) five letters. I think it far more likely that the cutter, nearing the end, and with an assistant calling out each letter to him, made a slip – forgot that '**R**' (as in lines 1 to 3) was supposed to be the half-uncial **R**, and cut the plain capital **R** to which he was long accustomed.

The upshot of this examination is not meant negatively, nor is to be read as uninformed criticism of previous workers. It is, nevertheless, that neither linguistic nor epigraphical factors provide detailed guidance as to date. Prima facie the inscription seems later than 500, mainly because of the small equal-armed cross with its expanded terminals (marginally, because the 'open R' seen in **TREMDUM** is probably after rather than before 500, on the strength of other inscriptions). The Group II, 7th to 9th century, bracket is so wide that it happens to contain the likely date; but this is in the 7th, not Jackson's preferred 8th century. The text's total reliance on the *editio vulgata*, Jerome's Vulgate Latin Bible, would probably favour a period not earlier than the 6th century; and, as far as can yet be stated, the typology of generated pictures (mental images) within the Welsh inscriptions would also place this no earlier than the 6th century.[35] In that combined light there is rather more freedom than might have been expected to put forward, on the basis of a purely historical model – an informed guess as to who the two men were and why they might have died here – the proposed date around the middle of the 7th century. That may be open to some criticism as being no better than a contextual 'date' or estimate. When we investigate the various ways in which many of these Insular inscriptions have, so far, been dated (or 'dated') it could well emerge that context is as sound a guide as any other approach.

Inscriptional Computus

The computus of any Biblical-style inscription is its entire mathematical side, distinct from literary and linguistic aspects. A computus is there anyhow; in the number of words (W) which from the 5th century, word separation having been abandoned, may be run together (*scriptura continua*) or carried over from one line to the next; in the number of syllables (S), most easily found by chanting aloud and ignoring elisions that would be normal in verse-scansion; and in the letters (L) counted visually as units of writing, graphs, for which purpose a numeral like XXXV, 35, contains four. (Not relevant here is a convention that two, or uncommonly three, letters ligatured, sharing cut strokes, are counted as a single letter.) There may also be a difference between counts of letters in the display (LD) and those of the original composition or model (LM), because LM can be reduced to LD by abbreviation – either suspension, omitting final letters as AVG(ustus), or contraction, those within a word as P(res)B(ite)R.

Originating well before 400 and in the secular world was an assignment to a 20-letter alphabet, ABCD EFGH ILMN OPQR STUX, of values; A B C D count as 1 2 3 4 and so on through to T U X 18 19 20. In this system, letters-as-numbers (LaN), other letters found in archaic Latin and Greek or Hebrew had to be assimilated, so K = C = 3; Y = (generally) I = 9 and Z = S = 17. These last three were used in a 23-letter ABC, for instance by Bede, and in British inscriptions after the 9th century the LaN basis changes to the 23-letter system.

Letters-as-numbers, LaN, must be distinguished from letters-as-numerals, LNu, the familiar Roman practice of using selected letters M D C L X V I to denote 1000, 500, 100, 50, 10, 5 and 1. Both systems occur and can be interlocked in a single computus. In the memorial *421 Rostece*, the girl's age is ANI XIII 'thirteen years' and the letter I, functioning separately as 'one', occurs 13 times in the display (similar repetitions are known in other memorials where age in years and/or months is shown).

Immediate study of a display text, aided if necessary by a rapid mental expansion to the underlying model, reveals certain signals (clues, hints, pointers) built-in deliberately to guide the reader to the interpretations. Three such signals, at least, should be detectable at once. Key numbers, low integers, usually come as two, though a single key number may suffice. These are numbers that either simplex (as themselves) or in multiple form occur throughout a computus far more frequently than chance should permit and transpire to have further specific use in devices, arrangements of letters or wording that do not appear in immediate display. Square numbers begin with four, basic indicator of a four-sided shape, and imply that as part of an interpretation some letters are to be set out, re-arranged, in a letter square of equal-length lines and columns. Triangular numbers arise from a series like this: $1 + 2 + 3 + 4 + 5 + 6 + 7 = 28$, where 28 is 'the triangular from 7', written $\Delta 7$ (of several formulae, an easy one is that the triangular from N is the sum of $\frac{1}{2}$(N-squared) plus $\frac{1}{2}$(N) – that from 12, from $\frac{1}{2}$ x 144 plus $\frac{1}{2}$ x 12, or 72 plus 6, will be 78). In computus, a whole range of non-successive triangulars may be given, the message being again that selected letters are meant to be triangularised, a process shortly to be demonstrated.

Apart from the sophisticated device of producing mental images, the equivalent of pictures (at first, ground-plans as seen from above) suggested by special disposition of lettering, the main purpose of square and triangularised re-arrangements was to offer new readings of letters – almost always reading downwards, strictly acrostics on the left or starting-side, telestichs if on the right (last column) and mesostichs if anywhere between.[36] In the Roman world acrostics were real readings, new words so formed, and certainly by the 4th century could be found not just in squares but in rectangular dispositions (grids). True acrostics can be found, in the background, within Insular inscriptions up to the early 11th century. However, commoner were what amounted to numerical acrostics; it is the added-up total value of the letters in a column, or the diagonal side of a triangle, that was needed to reinforce a key number, to show a number known to carry (Biblical) allusive or symbolic import, or to reproduce a figure representing the total value by LaN of some proper name. When this process began is not clear, but it can be found in the Vulgate (p.40 below).

The last computus feature to be mentioned concerns the ratio or proportion, the harmonious division of any aspects of text in a manner exhibiting a recognised ratio. Bisection into equal or almost-equal halves (division by mean ratio) is fairly simple. Division by extreme ratio (otherwise 'the Golden Mean', Divine or ideal proportions, etc.) reaches or approximates a ratio of 1 to 1·618, otherwise ·382 to ·618 of a whole. The constant 1·618, or Φ (phi), is generated by simple geometric figures and 'the Golden Mean' can be represented by a rectangle – of pleasing, harmonious, ideal or 'Divine' proportions – whose shorter and longer sides contain 1 and 1·618 units.[37]

Inclusion in a Biblical-style text of totals (W, S or L) that are divisible at an extreme section into extreme ratio is common also. Our mode of finding the extreme section of a total is of course calculator-multiplying by ·382 (or ·618) and rounding to the nearest whole figure. There is now consistent evidence that Insular authors (the composer of *986 Ioruert* among them) did not always calculate, but found extreme ratio from memorised sets of so-called Fibonacci numbers, the first being 1.2.3.5.8.13.21.34.55.89.144... . In these, each number from the third is the sum of the two preceding, and those two are in extreme ratio within their sum – the higher the numbers, the nearer to ·382 : ·618. Two non-Fibonacci sets, 5.7.12.19.31.50... (employed here), and 4.9.13.22.35.57..., were also known and used, certainly in Britain. We can assume that persons trained in this manner of composition knew their Fibonacci sets up to at least 1.8.9.17.26.43..., and all the triangulars up to at least 210, Δ20, by heart and had learned them as children under the head of *arithmetica* or *geometria*. (I do not digress now into this as part of the evidence for the continuation of Roman-style education, at all levels, long after 400 in parts of western and northern Britain.)

Suitably prepared by this (condensed) guide to computus we can now look at the inscription as if seeing it for the first time in, say, the year AD 700. Where are its key numbers? The first is **six**. There are **six** words before, **six** after, the Cross. There are 30, **six**-times-five, syllables. There are 72, twice **six**-squared, letters. **Six** (-UE, -N, -N-, -EN-) are lost by abbreviation, with a model (LM) therefore of 78, **six** times 13. The second key number must be **five**. The text has **five** lines. The first and last letters overall are I(n) ... (tremendu)M, 9.11 = **five**-times-four. In the display the four corner-letters are I₉ R₁₆ I₉ M₁₁, = **five**-times-nine. Of 20 possible letters, only **five**-times-three are used (no B F G H X here). The initials of the **five** lines, I₉ U₁₉ S₁₇ A₁ I₉, add up to 55. In the display, letter 'I' (as numeral one) can be found ten times, twice **five**. The two key numbers are also linked; for instance, syllables, 30 (**six**-times-**five**), and combined total of W 12, S 30 and LM 78 is 120 (**six**-times-**five**, times-four).

There are many triangular numbers, the most obvious being the full letter count of 78 at Δ12. Here are some others. The names IORUERT RUALLAUN contain 15 letters (Δ5) and their first and last letters are I and N, 9 and 12 = 21 (Δ6). With IN SINDONE MUTI added to IORUERT RUALLAUN we have 28 letters (Δ7). The number 36 – as it happens, crucial, and seen in the text when quartered (p.12 earlier) – appears, doubled, as LD of 72, and is both the square of key number **six** and Δ8. The corner-letters I R I M gave 45, which is Δ9. The five line-initials added to 55, which is Δ10. Last letters of both the first six words, N₁₂ E₅ I₉ T₁₈ E₅ S₁₇, and also the second six words, with I₉ M₁₁ T₁₈ N₁₂ E₅ M₁₁, add up to 66, which is Δ11. As the concept of 'square', the display itself is probably closer to a square than anything else. We have already had 36 as the square of six. The first, top, line has 16 (four-squared) letters, and its first and last are I$_9$ R$_{16}$, 25 or five-squared. In the display, letter 'D' with value of four appears four times.

The highest of the triangular numbers, 78 (letter count of the model text) as $\Delta12$, will serve to demonstrate the technique. There are two ways to re-arrange the suitable letters in triangular form; point upwards ('pyramid') and point downwards ('inverted'). Between them these provide quite a number of new LaN totals – up or down the diagonal sides; the horizontal top or bottom line; and the sum of the three letters at angles ('apicals'). There is an element of trial-and-error in finding triangularisation that yields allusive numbers or those relevant to the text – not all will – and though with practice it is possible to carry out triangularisations up to $\Delta6$ or $\Delta7$ entirely in the mind, by mental arithmetic, larger totals have to be written out (and must usually have been written out in the past). It can also be pointed out here that it is far easier to compose these triangles in Latin than it would be in English, to ensure that letters of required values are brought to the edges for addition. Flexibility of word-order, alternatives (IORUERT RUALLAUNQUE and not IORUERT ET RUALLAUN, or vice versa; ADUENTUM SPECTANT IN PACE TREMENDUM, not ADUENTUM TREMENDUM SPECTANT IN PACE) and even selective spellings (RUALLAUN, not RIUALLAUN; IORUERT, not IORUERTH), and the wealth of synonyms in Latin all contribute to this.

The intended triangularisation turns out to be the inverted:

```
 9      I N S I N D O N E M U T      18
 9        I I O R U E R T R U A       1
10         L L A U N Q U E S E        5
14           P U L C R I S I U        19
 4            D I C I I A D U         19
 5             E N T U M S P          14
 5              E C T A N T           18
 9               I N P A C            3
 5                E T R E             5
11                 M E N              12
 4                  D U               19
11                   M                11

96                                   144
```

Apicals, **I T M**, give a meaningless 38. As in the majority of such triangles the message resides in the side-totals (and note that letter **E**, value (key number) five, appears in them five times). The sum of 96 and 144 is 240, which is twice 120 (total of W, S and LM), and twice the product of (key number) six, by (key number) five, by (square) four – all the computus signals come together here. On the left, 96 is the value in total of the first-mentioned name, **IORUERT**, as 9.13.16.19.5.16.18 = 96; and in the top line we can find in the correct order the relevant vowels **I I O E**, and the final **-T**. On the right, 144 is the square of six (36), times 'the square', four; but it is more than that, and a familiar total in triangularisations from inscriptions with sufficient letters. It symbolises the Heavenly City, the abode of souls that await the Resurrection and the *iudicium*, Judgement, from various statements in Apocalypsis (Revelation) – 21.17, its wall of 144 cubits; 7.4, the number of those sealed as the elect, 144,000 (appropriately, for what follows here, twelve thousand each from the twelve tribes named from the Sons of Israel, Jacob).

It is common to find, within a computus, close links between square and triangular numbers. Much of this will be fortuitous. In the sequence 1–100 there are 10 squares and 12 triangulars, only 36 as 6-squared and Δ8 being common; in the sequence 1–200 these figures rise to 14 and 18 respectively. That means, crudely, that any number from 1 to 100 generated randomly has a not-quite 1-in-5 chance of being square or triangular, and from 1 to 200 a chance of 1-in-6·45. Where an element of design or purpose, beyond mere chance, must be suspected is the generation (by adding letter values) of numbers that are square, or triangular, or (with 36) both, but are also multiples of the key numbers in a computus. So far, in 25-plus inscriptions, key numbers ranging from 5 to 17 have been found and it is doubtful that lower or higher ones were used.

An example here starts by noticing that the five lines of text have different letter-lengths; in the display, 16.13.16.15.12 = 72. Since we are looking at five lines, we bear key number **five** in mind. Take the first **five** letters of each line to construct a square:

It has no verbal acrostic (mesostich, telestich, diagonal) readings. The corners I_9 N_{12} I_9 E_5 = 35, **five**-times-seven. The first column, we have already seen, adds to 55; so does the last (12.16.10.12.5). This is **five**-times-11; it is also triangular ($\Delta 10$), and from ten (**five**-times-two). We need not add up all the other possible totals. The shape has no significance but it combines a square, a triangular (twice) and key number **five** in a manner that strongly implies calculated inclusion. If it carries any message at all (doubtful) it would be that **five** is of particular importance or use at a subsequent moment (see p.42).

The second example does have some significance. From the text quartered, the letter count of quarters one and three proves to be 36, and thus to constitute a square which is that of a key number. It is also triangular. We look at both shapes:

```
              88
 9   I N S I N D O N   12        9              I                  9
 5     E M U T I I U   19       12            N S                 17
 4       D I C I I A    1        9          I N D                  4
 4         D U E N T   18       13        O N E M                 11
19           U M S P   14       19      U T I I U                 19
 5             E C T   18        4    D I C I I A                  1
 1               A N   12        4  D U E N T U M                 11
18                 T   18       17 S P E C T A N T                18
                                            88
65                    112       87                                90
```

At first glance this may not seem remarkable; but it is, and just as carefully contrived as the textual construction that allowed the letters of the two quarters to amount to 36 (and, for much more elaborate ends, to be the necessary letters). First, combined totals are $65 + 112 = 177$, and $87 + 90 = 177$; they are identical. Now in a triangularisation of this extent, the occurrence is (so far) unique, though facilitated because each triangle has 15 letters to add and, of each 15, eight are common (**A D D I N T U U**). Do they imply a special quality to these 36 letters, perhaps as a square? Second, both horizontals are identical as 88 (and the apicals of the pyramid I_9 S_{17} T_{18} are half of 88 as 44). But just as in the full triangularisation of 78 letters as $\Delta 12$, one side-total gave 96, the value of **IORUERT**, so here we add $R_{16} U_{19} A_1 L_{10} L_{10} A_1 U_{19} N_{12}$ ($= 88$) and find the second name. Does this further imply that whatever else can be shown by these 36 letters particularly concerns Ruallaun and (since his name-value was similarly given) Ioruert? Subsequent analysis will firmly support such beliefs.

What must not be forgotten is that these devices, with several others whose use will be demonstrated, are (in sum) no more than the mathematical adjuncts of Biblical-style composition. They are the tools of the trade required to unveil interpretations inherent in the words and letters and internal totals of the text but scarcely apparent in the immediate display. Their combined use in a Christian context, and no Insular inscription other than Christian can be found employing Biblical style, was driven by a very much older belief; that Number as an attribute of God stands outside Man and any of his works, informed the Creation and, being universal and all-pervading, must actually precede the Creation. Substituting 'Nature' for 'God' a modern reinforcement of the belief is the discovery that growth-forms containing Fibonacci number-sets occur in, e.g., plant life.[38] In this particular *986 Ioruert* text the use of extreme ratio is to validate, to affirm the authenticity of, various readings and anagrams where component letters are not consecutive (are 'split'). In others (*350 Idnert* is one), coincidence of three extreme sections, of W, S and L, highlights a particular name or word.[39] Not all of the identified Biblical-style texts, most of them from post-500 Wales, can be shown to generate mental images, implicit 'pictures' with explanatory labelling; but ten or more do so, *986 Ioruert* among them. In every instance the image must be generated by mathematical means.

The interpretations that follow take us to the Old Testament, and then to the Gospels; separated intellectual constructs, they are inevitably linked by their common base of 78, or 36, letters and by the doctrine that part of the NT is the fulfilment of much of the OT. In the maze that follows the thread to grasp is offered by a first glance at the stone itself, **twelve** words, **one** central Cross – for the OT, Jacob-Israel and his Sons; for the NT, Christ and His Disciples. All else proceeds from this double equation.

Interpretation: The Old Testament

It would be daunting – and certainly beyond my powers – to attempt any summary of theological teaching in Wales at this period; but one would suppose that perception of the Bible as the Word in bipartite form was long entrenched. Gildas tells us[40] that he had 'gazed on these things and many others in the Old Testament as though on a mirror *reflecting our own life*; then I turned to the New Testament also, and read there more clearly what had previously, perhaps, been dark to me...' and the italicised words will remind us that the *986 Ioruert* author may have taken over, from the Preface to DEB, the image of suffering and tribulations of a particular group of Britons as a repetition of the God-ordained punishments inflicted upon the Children of Israel.

But the whole text is, like the Bible, two-fold; with its (near-symmetrical) division by the little cross. The opening **IN SINDONE MUTI** directs readers to the Gospel, more closely to that portion of Matthew that also describes a death and burial. In that setting, twelve words disposed around the Cross at once suggests allusion to the twelve Disciples (named in Matthew 10) around Jesus. That does not touch a parallel interpretation; twelve named sons of Jacob-who-was-Israel personified, tribal eponyms, around the patriarch. As the first three words reduce the NT allusion to the gospels alone, so this second figure contains OT allusion to the Pentateuch, the first Five Books of Moses.

And here, at once, verbal and numerical pointers emerge in plenty, The first two initials I(*n*) S(*indone*) are those of ISrahel. The Cross is marked, preceded by the same letters – (*sepulcr*) IS +. From the twelve word-initials, two before and two following the Cross, (I S M I) R S I A (S I P T), are the first four letters of ISRA*hel*. *Sepulcris* may be abl. plur. and exhibit the post-classical spelling without –h– (*sepulc(h)rum*), but, matching the *sepulchrum* of Christ, the burial-niche in Joseph of Arimathia's *monumentum*, we have the far earlier burial of Moses; like the grave of medieval Arthur, where *anoeth bid bet y arthur*[41] strikes me as directly inspired by Deuteronomy 34.6, the *sepulchrum* of Moses in some valley in the land of Moab as a wonder – *et non cognovit homo sepulchrum eius usque in praesentem diem* 'and no man knoweth, unto this day, his grave'.

An obvious numerical reference to Moses is his age at death (Deut. 34.7 'he was an hundred and twenty years when he died'), and it is immediately given by a common computus-device, the combined total of words (12), syllables (30) and letters (78). It confirms, with the various IS(rahel) pointers, where interpretation must start. Because the name of Jacob, $I_9 A_1 C_3 O_{13} B_2$ adds up to 28, the triangular number from 7, and then because it can be seen that the first five words of the inscription (omitting enclitic -que) contain 28 letters, a connection would be suspected. Perhaps, momentarily, the words can stand for the Five Books as the principal repository of the story of Jacob's descendants before the Promised Land. The rapid triangularisation of those 28 letters produces

9	**I N S I N D O**	13
12	**N E M U T I**	9
9	**I O R U E**	5
16	**R T R U**	19
1	**A L L**	10
1	**A U**	19
12	**N**	12
60		**87**

– the meaning of which is seen when 60 and 87 are added (=**147**). For this is from Genesis 27.48, a second reference (as for Moses) to age-at-death; 'the whole age of Jacob, **147** years'. As if to confirm it, we look again at the 12 word-initials that contain **I S** and then **R S I A**; because $I_9 S_{17} M_{11} I_9 R_{16} S_{17} I_9 A_1 S_{17} I_9 P_{14} T_{18}$ also add up to 147.[42]

With this, any reader knowing the Bible fully would discern that we have begun with the OT, and that Ruallaun and Ioruert are being retrojected into the Pentateuch, the company of the Sons of Jacob-who-is-Israel. And a particular light would dawn; for the inscription's twelve words are, obviously, those Sons.

IN	beniam **I N**
SINDONE	**S Y** m **E O N**
MUTI	zab **U** lon
IORUERT	**I O** s **E** ph
RUALLAUNQUE	**R U** b **E N**
SEPULCRIS	**L E U I**
IUDICII	**I U D** a
ADUENTUM	g **A D**
SPECTANT	d **A N**
IN	**I** sachar
PACE	**A** ss **E** r
TREMENDUM	**N E** p **T** hali **M**

The list comes from Exodus 1.2–5. When **RUALLAUNQUE** is paired with Ruben (Jerome's spelling; Greek Roubēn) we know that Ruben was the first-born (*primogenitus*, Genesis 46.8), as Ruallaun was the father; in placing him next to **IORUERT**-Ioseph we recall that it was Ruben among the brethren who caused Joseph's life to be spared, when he was next delivered into exile in Egypt.

Placing Benjamin, youngest of the Sons, in top position may have been deliberate if Gildas's broad parallel in matching the 'tribes' of the Britons with the suffering Tribes of Israel was being followed. The author's 7th-century spelling of the name of Ruallaun's kingdom would almost certainly been *Brecheniauc*, today the modern 'Brycheiniog'.[43] Observe that the first five letters in BENIA (min) are to be seen in (B r E che N I A uc). Can this be dismissed as coincidence? Key number six is still involved. RUBEN adds to 54, six-times-nine, IOSEPH to 66, six-times-11; and their sum repeats that Mosaic total of 120. Further, the composition is a memorial to Ruallaun-Ruben and Ioruert-Ioseph, in which the twelve words (names, Sons) are divided, six and six. Where else in the OT may this be found? Exodus 28.9 onwards relates God's command to Moses about the making of the accoutrements for the robes of Aaron as high priest. 'And take thou two stones of onyx, and scribe on them the names of the Sons of Israhel'. The disposition comes in v.10, 'six names on the one stone, and the six remaining on the other, according to the order of their birth'. That order, elsewhere starting with Ruben-Symeon-Leui-Iuda and ending with 'little Benjamin' was not followed in the table of words-as-names and could not be followed in what is shown now, but our author managed to repeat the six-and-six division – on a slab that, for a moment (Fig.3), becomes *duo lapides onychini* – by using the last letters of the 12 words:

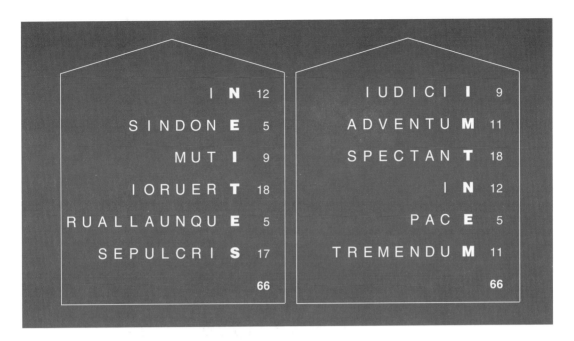

Fig. 3   *Twelve words as 'two onyx tablets'*

The columns are equalised, by the last-letter LaN. The sums are again six-divisible. The total, 132, is eleven-times-twelve; and looking back at Exodus 1.2–5, we find eleven of the Sons named together, and then as the twelfth, Joseph 'who was in Egypt already'.

As the current interpreter of this startling inscription, and of many like it (a few, equally complex), I have the advantage of several years' work in re-discovering the methodology and content of 'inscriptional' Biblical style as a mode of composition; and am, consequently, no longer surprised at anything in this field. Yet I can appreciate its total unfamiliarity to those meeting it for the first time, the impact of the necessary mathematics (though in truth the *arithmetica* is simple and elementary) and the inevitable scepticism that will be aroused. My hope is that the rapid-fire narration of these allusions, totals, letter-values and other devices (tied, as they demonstrably are, to a Latin version of the Bible that all may consult, and that most of us may wish we knew better) carries a cumulative effect; of credibility as well as of acceptability. It works, and therefore it is real. The message thereby conveyed is, in a Biblical sense, apposite to the composer's intentions. His Old Testament figure overall places two named men in a *mise-en-scène* that may be utterly un-historical but which he believed to be spiritually appropriate.

There is a further stage. To discuss it is to risk a slight circularity of argument in that, having opened with a model that supposed Ruallaun and Ioruert to have been father and son, one might look like buttressing that supposition by adducing a very much older father-and-son connection. Nevertheless still in the OT we may next find a personal lament for the two dead men; something that (circularity again) might lend support to the idea of a close or immediate family link between the author and the commemorated.

The author becomes for a brief space *Dauid*, David the singer and harper before his elevation as the great King. As such an Apollo-figure we have seen his claims. He created the text as a hexametric couplet, produced chiasmus, quartered the text and showed his mastery of Latin and knowledge of the Scriptures. David sang his lament for a father and his son. Ruallaun, Ruben, is now Saul, and Ioruert, Ioseph, becomes Ionathan. Key number six continues to inform us and to control interpretation (as, coincidentally, it does in many of the crucial OT phrases – David's words, II Samuel 1.26, *doleo super te frater me Ionathan*, are six words, twice six syllables). Whether one takes r **UAL** laun = s **AUL** or rual **LAU** n = s **AUL**, the common letters are three; add three from **IO** ruer **T** = **IO** na **T** han. Indeed the first name, twice a king's and twice a father's, can be found within the text as a split and validated reading. It requires the first 36 (six-times-six) letters, so:

in	2		
s		1	S
indonemutiioruertru	19		
A		1	A
lla	3		
U		1	U
nquesepu	8		
L		1	L
	32	4	

and the validation, evidence that these are not just letters picked at random, is proper to the citation of a name. **SAUL** (4) occupies one-ninth of the 36-letter span or, put another way, the ratio of the span to the un-used letters, 36:32 is 9:8, epogdous (see p.42). Then, since in the reality of the 7th-century burial at Llanllywenfel two bodies covered with one shroud (*sindone*) lay as two burials (*sepulcris*) marked with one slab that (treated as the onyx tablets) could be dual, we have the six-word epitaph that any ancient, and many a modern, reader will think of: II Samuel 1.23, *in morte quoque non sunt divisi* 'in death moreover they were not divided'.

It is to another 36 letters, those of the first and third quarters of the text (p.11) that we now finally turn; observing that their words, **IN SINDONE MUTI / IUDICII ADUENTUM SPECTANT**, might apply to any (plural) subject, OT and NT, as burials where disembodied souls await the day of reckoning that must follow the coming of the Messiah or the second coming of the Redeemer at the Resurrection. Triangles we have seen. Thirty-six happens to be triangular (as $\Delta 8$; p.38 below) but here the letters are to be disposed as a square:

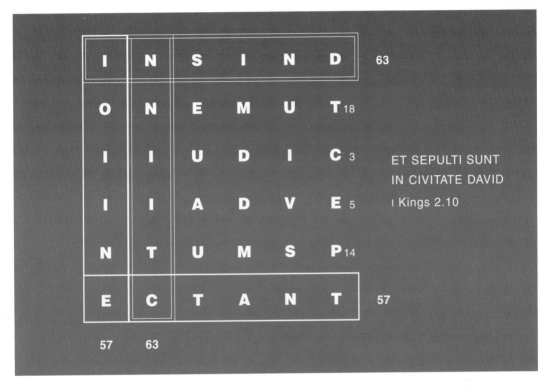

Fig. 4   *Devised plan, David's City of Jerusalem*

In such cases, judging by the results apparent in similar devices of earlier date (*421 Rostece*, c.500[44]) and later (*350 Idnert*, 806, the first devised-profile image[45]), readers who had already scratched out the letter square on a slate or tablet – it is a step too far removed from the display to be resolved mentally – would rapidly add up the values of the six lines and the six columns, noting the totals, the aim being to identify those that were equal. Here the results (outlined) begin to suggest that we have a plan. If so, from the device of the letter square we are generating a mental image (a devised plan) and it may represent an idea, much stylised, of David's royal city of Jerusalem – not its Heavenly counterpart as described with abundant details and dimensions in Apocalypsis, but the historic Late Bronze Age settlement over which king David ruled (Fig.4).

Plainly we are still in the same Old Testament world of the Pentateuch and the historical books. Columns 1 and 2 each with six letters echo the two tablets of onyx with six names each, and their values 57 and 63 again produce the figure of 120. On the right, column 6, letters T_{18} C_3 E_5 P_{14} give 40, all the years of David's reign; seven before, and 33 during, his rule in this city, the larger period being repeated in the NT as Christ's earthly years. To their left ('within the City') **U D I** over **A D U**, six letters, provide the anagram of **DAUID**. When David died he was buried within the city; I Kings 2.10, *et sepultus est in ciuitate Dauid* (six words, 12 syllables, 28 letters). Anachronistically, Ruallaun and Ioruert are shown here as well; read upwards in column 3 to see, with DAUID, letters **U A** (R **UA** llaun) and **U E** (Ior **UE** rt). We could change the Vulgate sentence slightly to read *et sepulti sunt* (plural) *in ciuitate Dauid*. Those 28 letters involve the eleven, **A C D E I L N P S T U**. In the 24 letters that make up the right-side two-thirds of the square, we could find the words as anagrams except for the **L** in *sepuLti*, from **A C D E I M N P S T U**. Quite possibly as one continues to explore Fig.4 further devices and allusions would be revealed. For the moment, what has been listed above can suffice. The author has told us, with clarity and in abundance, what he wished all and any readers to know on this score.

Interpretation: The New Testament

The twelve-word three-line memorial, now sadly in fragments, to *Idnert filius Iacobi* (*350 Idnert* = ECMW no.116), at Llanddewi-brefi was composed by the dead man's father (OW Iago, latinised *Iacobus*) and carries an internal chronogram of DCCCVI, AD 806. By a series of logical steps and demonstrations the text leads to a final picture, not a true devised-profile image but the imposition of 64 letters and 11 interval-blanks as a row of five-by-five squares on a full Crucifixion scene. Showing Christ on Calvaria-Golgotha, flanked by the two thieves, Sponge-bearer and Lance-wielder and with sun and moon above, it must represent a lost Gospel miniature – probably Continental and of *c*.800 – on the lines of the Rabbula Gospel's little paintings of AD 586. Very detailed labelling of the scene, using the text, is all from Matthew 27. Iago's purpose was to show his son on Christ's right being crucified in the guise of Dismas, one of the two *latrones* named in the Apocryphal NT Acts of Pilate.

When analysing and then publishing *350 Idnert* [46] I did not see (and the density of this text with its computus can perhaps excuse my omission) that the twelve words are also the twelve Disciples' names from Matthew 10, much as we have seen the words of *986 Ioruert* already portrayed as the names of Jacob's Sons. Here is the table:

HIC	I o H annes	**HI**
IACET	IAC obus alph E i	**IACE** *
IDNERT	s I mo N p ETR us	**INERT**
FILIUS	ph ILI pp US	**ILIUS** *
IACOBI	IACOB us	**IACOB** *
QUI	thadde U s	**U**
OCCISUS	IU da S i SC ari O tes	**OCISSU**
FUIT	ma T the U s publ I canus	**UIT**
PROPTER	ba RT h O lom E us	**ROTE**
PREDAM	A n DRE as	**REDA**
SANCTI	SI mo N CA naneus	**SANCI**
DAUID	thom A s DID ym U s	**DAUID**

Column 1 gives the text, column two the names from Matthew 10; in the third column, letters used in 2 are repeated in the order that they occur in 1 (starred cases, in the same order). The text has 64 letters, 49 of which (77 percent) are used. In the equations Iago puts himself against a senior figure, James son of Zebedee, brother of the evangelist John; and his son against none other than Simon Peter. (Note how *occisus* 'slain, murdered' goes with Judas Iscariot.)

Llanddewi-brefi, an ancient (6th-century) monastic church to St David, Dewi Sant, stands by the headwaters of the Teifi in Cors Garon and is just within the kingdom of Ceredigiaun, Cardigan. As post-Roman crows flew, it is only 18 miles west of Llanllywenfel though somewhat further by tracks across the hills. My impression is not so much that Iago — abbot of Llanddewi-brefi at the time? — and our Llanllywenfel author were schooled in the same arcane tradition but that the former knew of, and in several ways imitated the work of, the latter. We have seen the table with Jacob's sons. We can now turn to its New Testament equivalent, also using Matthew 10:

IN	I oha N nes	IN *
SINDONE	SI m ON p E trus	SIONE *
MUTI	M a T the U s publ I canus	MUTI
IORUERT	ba RT h O lom EU s	ORUET
RUALLAUNQUE	th A *DD* EU s	UAE
SEPULCRIS	SI mon C anan EUS	SEUCIS
IUDICII	IUD as I s C ar I otes	IUDICI *
ADVENTUM	AND r E as	ADEN
SPECTANT	i AC obu S alph E i	SECA
IN	I acobus	I
PACE	P hillippus	P
TREMENDUM	T ho M as D idy MU s	TMDUM

In this case, excluding the geminated **LL–DD** match, 46 of 76 letters (61 percent) are used again, thrice in the same order. However, it is not unkind to point out that Bartholomeus and Thaddeus cannot be reckoned among the more prominent of the Disciples. The purpose of the demonstration, one that would have been suggested by the earlier table with the Twelve Sons, cannot have been primarily or exclusively to elevate the memory of the two dead men. I suggest that it served to move the focus of interpretation from the Old Testament to the New, at the same time indicating which Gospel (Matthew's) would form the reference-basis. But this takes us back to the starting point, **IN SINDONE MUTI** alongside Matthew 27.59 *involvit illud sindone munda*; to fresh perception of the display as twelve words/Disciples, clustered around their central Cross/Christ; and thence to a realisation that what can be seen immediately upon the face on the stone is itself a mental image, a 'picture' to be generated by the viewer's own mind, and technically a display plan (Fig.5). The area of the lettering, slightly rhomboidal but able to pass for a square, is the ground-plan of the *monumentum*, the rock-cut cave outside Jerusalem's walls belonging to Joseph of Arimathia and first used as Christ's tomb. Anticipating the description in Matthew 27, we see that line 3 marks an internal space; the **S** of **S**(*epulcris*), the *saxum magnum* or great stone that closed the entrance; the Cross, the Body of Christ; and in **SE p U lcr IS** the label, **SEUIS**, split anagram of

IESUS. This is a guide, a signpost, a powerful clue or pointer, to return to the 36-letter square that served as a plan of David's Jerusalem. Now it takes on a New Testament meaning and, as a start, confirms its 36, six-squared, reality thrice. Corner letters I$_9$ D$_4$ E$_5$ T$_{18}$ make 36; so do the four Is (each = 9) making the blocking-stone. As numerals they are also IIII – *quatuor* 'four', a square, and could even represent four (disjoined) equal sides of a real, drawn square. Fig.6 is a plan of the *monumentum*, the resting place of the Crucified Lord. It is the author's model of nothing less than the Holy Sepulchre, and he proposes to place Ioruert and Ruallaun within it. After centuries of oblivion we are now enabled to see exactly how he accomplished this.

Fig. 5 *Display plan of Joseph of Arimathia's* monumentum

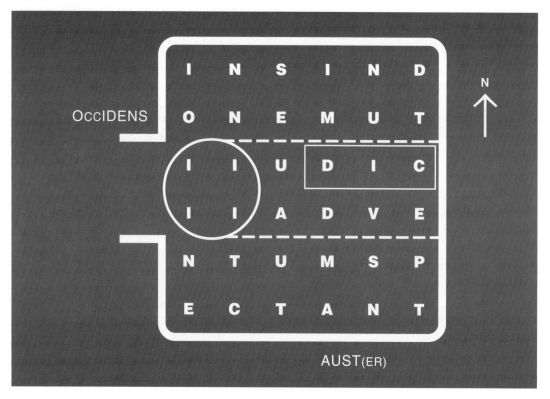

Fig. 6 *Devised plan, the* monumentum *and the Holy Sepulchre*

The labelling of the image, mostly from Matthew 27 and 28, was meticulously planned and is wholly apposite. It is controlled by key number six. Lines 1 and 2 with their twice-six letters, **INSIND / ONEMUT**, cover the *monumentum* as the larger and embracing feature. From Matthew 27.59–60, we take the six words *Ioseph [posuit] in monumento suo novo*, descriptive of the main event. Each can be found as a part-anagram in the twelve letters (below, 7/9 means 'seven of nine letters can be found'):

IOSEPH	I . S . . .	MONUMENTO	. N . . . .
(4/6)	O . E . . .	(7/9)	O N E M U T
POSUIT	. . S I . .	SUO	. . S . . .
(5/6)	O . . . U T	(3/3)	O . . . U .
IN	I N . (IN) .	NOUO	. N . . . .
(2/2)	. . . . . .	(3/4)	O . . . U .

The six words contain 30, six-times-five, letters; and of these, 24, six-times-four, 80 percent, occur as part-anagrams.

With lines 5 and 6, **NTUMSP/ECTANT**, it is at once obvious that (27.61) SEPULCHRUM
will be included and it seems likely that a second 30 letters from the text are to be used.
Selecting those that strike me as the most relevant, I propose (27.60) *exciderat in* PETRA,
(27.63) Christ's claim *post tres dies* RESURGAM, and (28.2) the appearance of the angel,
ANGELUS *enim Domini descendit*.

PETRA	. . . . . P	SEPULCHRUM	. . U M S P	
(4/5)	E . T A . .	(6/10)	E C	
RESURGAM	. . U M S .	ANGELUS	. . U . S .	
(5/8)	E . . A . .	(5/7)	E . . A N .	

In this instance, of the 30 letters PETRA.SEPULCHRUM.RESURGAM.ANGELUS we find
20 (66 percent) used in the part-anagrams; fewer, but I cannot guarantee, *sepulchrum* apart,
that these were all intended.

There is an intriguing hint here of recourse to extra-Biblical tradition. We may be in seventh-
century Wales, but within a world of literacy and scholarship. The few surviving accounts by
Western pilgrims to the Holy Land imply a channel along which quite detailed descriptions of
the major sites in post-400 Jerusalem could reach western Britain.[47] From Matthew 27 our
author could deduce a burial-cave, allowably quadrangular, cut in the rock, closed by a large
stone that (*advolvit*; 28.2, *revolvit*) should have been circular; and containing within it
a specific feature described as *sepulchrum*. On Iona later in the same century, the castaway
bishop Arculf was able to give Adomnán a mass of detailed, first-hand, descriptions and
apparently to draw for him various ground-plans with full verbal labelling.[48] Here, in our
Llanllywenfel ground-plan – 'labelled' in a rather different fashion – an assumption that its
vertical axis represents north-south, like most modern plans, is by no means always warranted
for the 7th century.[49] But (line 6) the letter **A**, with **U S T** adjoining it, could well be *aust(er)*,
aust(ralis) 'south' and (line 2, initial) **O**, with **I N** adjoining and **D E S** present in lines
1 and 2, similarly *o(cc)idens* 'west'. Exigencies of the text have placed the entrance and its
saxum magnum, **I I I I**, on the west, whereas there is some evidence from Arculf's and other
accounts that the *ostium* of the Holy Sepulchre was thought to face east.[50] However, one
passage in *De Locis Sanctis* (the true sense of which is not entirely clear)[51] states that within
the *monumentum*, really a cave (*speleum sive spelonca*), was the *sepulchrum* proper; in the
northern portion (*aquilonali parte*) of the *monumentum*. Here the body was laid on a kind

of inner hollow of *septem pedum* '7 feet' in length, a body-size rock pallet (*lectum*). It was the actual burial; *Domino Iesu Christo in ea sepulto* 'with Lord Jesus Christ … in it'.

We can think of this, and the possibility that some account similar to Arculf's was known to the author, when we look closely at lines 3 and 4; central interior, that part closed by the *saxum magnum*. Is it entirely without significance that we find the letters **D I C** – *D(ominus) I(esus) C(hristus)* – set out on line 3, northern of the two lines, and that **D – C**, 4.3 = 7, appears to give an east-west length? We have here eight letters; **..UDIC / ..ADUE**. Add them in four two-letter columns; 20, 8, 28 and 8. Their total is 64, square of eight, the *sepulchrum* proper as a square within a square. And one can surely read all the overlapping meanings now – **D C**, or **D D C**, for *deposita corpora* 'the bodies placed within', or (28.2) **A E D D C** *angelus enim Domini … de caelo* 'an angel of the Lord, from Heaven' seen by the two Mary's; but, most specifically, next to Christ's body, **U A**, for (r)UA(llaun), and **U E**, for (ior)UE(rt). Most of this of course comes directly from the author's labelling-source, the Vulgate Matthew (though this is an opportunity to stress that whether or not older, vetus Latina, Biblical versions were still in circulation there is abundant evidence from several Insular inscriptions of access to a Vulgate not a whit inferior to the oldest and fullest surviving MSS[52]). I believe, however, that we should not overlook a chance of the author's limited use of written material outside the canonical scriptures, or the suggestions that such might have been coming into southern Wales since the late 5th century.

Arguably this was the most impressive feat of all; to take six words that make perfect sense together, to show them as a 36-letter square and then, separately distinguishing the Old and New Testament applications, to construct a square that can be simultaneously David's Jerusalem and the Holy Sepulchre but using precisely the same letters as labels or components proper to the two different images. Christian our author certainly was, but human enough to tell us (shortly) his name. Meanwhile there is yet one more feature here to be described, for which (momentarily) we must look beyond the Gospel according to Matthew, though referring closely still to the plan in Fig.6.

The central lines – $I_9 \, I_9 \, U_{19} \, D_4 \, I_9 \, C_3 = 53$, and $I_9 \, I_9 \, A_1 \, D_4 \, U_{19} \, E_5 = 47$, together add to one hundred. In other inscriptions this may be taken to symbolise the Lost Sheep Saved, from the parable in Matthew 18; clearly that would be inappropriate where two souls are involved. What we have is a reference to another facet of the post-Crucifixion happenings, the anointing of Christ's Body and the story of Nicodemus in John's Gospel (3.2; 7.50; 19.39). This man, *ex Pharisaeis, princeps Iudaeorum*, depicted by John as an intellectual convert in secret, brought to Joseph of Arimathia *mixturam murrae et aloes quasi libras centum* 'a mixture of myrrh and aloes, as it might be an hundred pounds in weight', a costly tribute for the anointing of the corpse.

The lines 3-plus-4 total of 100 refers to this; and in the 12 letters of lines 2 and 3, O N E M U T I I U D I C , we find eight of the nine letters of 'Nicodemus' (ONEMUIDC = NICODEMUs). Line 2 contains . . . MU . for the *murrae*, line 4 has . . A . . E for the *aloes*. The last letters of lines 3 and 4 are C E; and the first four letters of line 5, as N T U M, complete *centum*, 100. There is no particular clue as to why this reference from a second gospel should be included, unless (John 3.1) Nicodemus as a *princeps* was thought appropriate in a memorial to two *principes* of the Britons. The inclusion seems certain and we might observe that the ratio (letter counts) of NICODEMUS, 9, to ONEMUIDC, 8 – epogdous, 9:8 ratio – is otherwise linked to the provision of proper names (p.42). (In view of what will be written about devices and totals built into Jerome's Vulgate translation – p.39 further – it is also worth commenting that $N_{12}I_9C_3O_{13}D_4E_5M_{11}U_{19}S_{17}$ adds to 93, and that John 19.39 *venit autem et Nicodemus qui venerat ad Iesum nocte primum ferens mixturam murrae et aloes quasi libras centum* (no MS variants here) takes up 93 letters.)

Triangularisation to Affirm Proper Names: A Source ?

We have already seen how triangles may be used to give totals that represent the LaN values of proper names – Iacob (= 28) and his age at death (= 147), Ruallaun (=88) and Ioruert (=96) are among such demonstrations. The earliest Insular use of the device is in *479 Cunaide*, Hayle, west Cornwall,[53] where particular stress was laid on the value-total of 53 ($C_3U_{19}N_{12}A_1I_9D_4E_5$ = 53) as if to affirm that the name, feminine and probably Irish,[54] was to be written thus and in no other manner (e.g., the expected *Cunaida). Initials of the first 5 words in this 13-word memorial, HIC PACE NVP(er) REQVIEVIT CVNAIDE, 8.14.12.16.3, yield 53; the display text contains for letters-as-numerals XXXX and thirteen Is, 40 + 13 = 53; and triangularisation of the model 66-letter text, as $\Delta 11$, gives inverted side-totals of 124 + 141 = 265 = 53 x 5.

Guided selection of letter sequences within textual inscriptions whose totals are triangulars is quite common but the usual purpose was to produce, from one or both diagonal sides, allusive numbers; mostly 33 (= 'a Christian death', Christ's earthly span), 100 ('the Lost Sheep Saved'), 144 ('soul in the Heavenly City') and 153 ('in the Net of God's redeeming grace'[55]). Here, interestingly, the figure of 88 given twice from the 36 letters of the square, as $\Delta 8$, for the LaN value of the inscribed **RUALLAUN** may (as with the earlier CVNAIDE, value 53) underline the particular spelling. It could have been written as RIUALLAUN, or even RIUALLON, neither of which would suit this inscription's interlocking computus.

Repetition of individual names in this roundabout manner is not likely to have been inherited from secular Roman practice, because names (and words) could be shown directly as acrostics (mesostichs, telestichs), as they are in the Lullingstone Europa mosaic couplet,[56] and because nominal orthography in Latin is generally fixed. Avitus (Lullingstone) and Viola in *393 Carausius* do not have alternative spellings. However, it is at least possible that this combination of nominal LaN values, totals from triangularisation and also totals from straight counting originated in the Vulgate, and was adopted thence into Insular practice before 500. The evidence comes from the passage of Matthew that provides the labelling for the Holy Sepulchre image, a passage also used to label the final depiction in *350 Idnert*[57] and presumably known by heart to the respective authors who (we could well assume) also understood its computus. Matthew 27.59–60 exists without MS variants in the primary codices of the Vulgate and can be taken to represent in precise detail what Jerome constructed and dictated. It comprises six clauses:

> et accepto corpore
> Ioseph involvit illud sindone munda
> et posuit illud in monumento suo novo
> quod exciderat in petra
> et advolvit saxum magnum ad ostium monumenti
> et abiit

Jerome guarantees the self-contained nature of the passage, ending as it does typically with an abrupt perfect (*abiit*), twice. First, there is a six-fold parallelism:

i	et accepto corpore Ioseph	A	E	P	T	
ii	involvit illud					
iii	sindone munda	S	N	M	U	A
iv	et posuit illud	O	S	U	I	T
v	in monumento suo novo					
vi	quod exciderat	E	I	A	T	
i'	in petra	P	E	T	A	
ii'	et advolvit					
iii'	saxum magnum	S	A	U	M	N
iv'	ad ostium	O	S	T	I	U
v'	monumenti					
vi'	et abiit	E	A	I	T	

Second, at the breakpoint, the line, there is a dual extreme-ratio division. The first part has 17 words and 38 syllables, the second 11 words and 23 syllables. The words are as $11:17 \rightarrow 61$, from the (Fibonacci) set 1.5.6.11.17.28.45..., and the syllables from a higher set, being $23:38 \rightarrow 61$, from 1.7.8.15.23.38.61.99... .

There are 143 letters here. The word-count of 28 is of course triangular, $\Delta 7$. One cannot triangularise words as such but one can use their initials. Here is the resultant inverted form:

5	E A C I I I S	17
11	M E P I I M	11
17	S N Q E I	9
14	P E A S	17
11	M A O	13
11	M E	5
1	A	1
70		**73**

The side-totals together repeat that figure of 143. Plainly it has relevance, but to what or whom? The subject of Jerome's passage, the wealthy pious Christian *decurio* (so Mark 15.43) who rescued the Body of Christ, is named in the specific form *ab* (not *ex*, or *de*) *Arimathia*. Matthew 27.57 has: *venit quidam homo dives ab Arimathia nomine Ioseph* – and this produces

$A_1 B_2$	3
$A_1 R_{16} I_9 M_{11} A_1 T_{18} H_8 I_9 A_1$	74
$I_9 O_{13} S_{17} E_5 P_{14} H_8$	66
	143

with, predictably, the total of 143 for a third time.

Our present order of the Gospels, Matthew Mark Luke John, may not be that in which Jerome revised or re-translated them and I suspect that the complex Matthew arrangement may have been preceded by partial trials. The corresponding passage in Mark (15.43–44) is:

> venit Ioseph ab Arimathia nobilis decurio
> qui et ipse erat expectans regnum Dei
> et audacter introiit ad Pilatum
> et petiit corpus Iesu
> Pilatus autem mirabatur si iam obisset

This also has 28 words (though triangularisation of their initials gives 153 or (pyramid) 113, not 143); but though printed as above from the Stuttgart edition there is a known variant from A (Amiatinus) of *petit* for *petiit*. If *introiit* is similarly condensed to *introit*, both readings being quite classical, the letter count falls from 145 to 143 and is the same value of (line 1) *Ioseph ab Arimathia*.

Jerome chose to cast his Matthew 27 passage as a parallelism. It could as easily have been worded chiastically, abcdef–f'e'd'c'b'a', and any competent Latinist could still rewrite it in that form. I mention this because not-really-parallel words, like *sindone munda* and *saxum magnum*, the former with a full vowel range i-o-e-u-a, the latter with paired a-u, a-u, are 'padded out' by shared letters; S N M U A, then S A U M N. This is frequent in the Pentateuch and Gospels both in parallel and chiastic settings. Does this suggest a Vulgate origin for the occurrence in a great many Insular inscriptions of what can be called inscriptional chiasmus; where, because of the paucity of words, pairings of original and then inverted chiastic terms have to be reinforced by shared or common letters? We have already seen earlier (p.11) the shape this takes in the Llanllywenfel text. Here it is from an earlier (*c.*500?) Welsh memorial, *421 Rostece*, Llanerfyl:

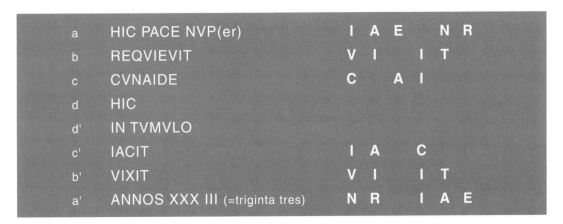

and similarly from the Cornish inscription, *479 Cunaide*:

In these and other chiastic arrangements the paired terms may be similar parts of speech (*requievit/vixit*) or thematically linked (*nuper/annos XXXIII*, time-general/time-specific), but the 'shared' letters' chiasmus is a feature lasting until the 11th century.[58] It does occur in Jerome's Vulgate and it may be that the Vulgate usage, minor though this was, inspired it.

The Author

It is time to meet the composer of the memorial; scribe of the putative five-line model and latinist responsible for so many complex references and images. There are preliminary clues to the name. As key number **six** provided the control for the OT and NT realisation, and the purpose of triangulars and squares becomes apparent, we are left with key number **five** not so far utilised. Letter E, value of five, may be the initial. Auctorial self-reference in longer Insular Latin writings, as David Howlett shows,[59] often follows a ratio from the mathematical basis of musical harmony, Greek *epogdous*, 9:8, with components (syllables) of a name placed one-ninth from the start and one-ninth from the end. The display text has 72 letters. Count in eight, I N S I N D O N and we face letter E. The full text, 78, closer to 81; count back nine, M U D N E M E R T and we face E a third time.

In the more elaborate of the post-600 Welsh inscriptions, authors' names are, by modern standards, encrypted (usually several times) but through devices that must have been expected and accepted and, when spotted, 'de-coded' without much difficulty. Commonest is the one called 'precession-and-interval', derived from the popular acrostics of the Roman world; letters of a name occur within a text, in the right order, separated either by equal or regular intervals – this is simply an acrostic or telestich in linear guise – or else by irregular, incremental, intervals taken from an extreme ratio set that has been used elsewhere in the composition. An additional element of concealment may be that a reading of a name must be made backwards. If so, and this does seem to be a Welsh invention no earlier than the 7th century, the implied command 'read this part backwards' comes from readily-apparent split and validated anagrams of Latin *rursus*, or *retrorsum*, or even both.

Here, we observe closely the inscription's first five words and notice **RETRORSUM** without much difficulty:

in / **S** ind **O** n **E MUT** i io **R** ue **R** t **R** / uallaunque

as **SOEMUTRRR** is re-arranged to give the word. Validation comes from the (non-Fibonacci) convention 5.7.12.19.31.50…, perhaps hinted at by key number five and the

12-word text. There are 31 letters above, the anagram-span having 19 letters, with (2 + 10 =) 12 left over. The relevant passage must now be set out backwards, *retrorsum*, when we see that it begins with letter e; intervals of five can be used:

E uqnua **L** laurt **R** euroi **I** / tumenodnisni = **ELRI**

(and there is the same validation; 12 unused, span of 19, total 31). One more interval, with reading **ELRIO**, would mean a division into 25 and 6, but 6:25 → 31, unlike 12:19 → 31, is not in extreme ratio. In any event the result of this, the first backwards reading, is replicated in a simpler first forwards reading, using word no.**6**; **SEPULCRIS**. Just as earlier this was used to provide a split anagram **S E p U l c r I S, SEUIS = IESUS**, so it offers (in the right order) **s E p u L c R I s = ELRI** as a split reading, with 1.4.5.9.14.23… to validate it.

For the name itself, which may not be previously attested but is entirely acceptable as (Archaic) Old Welsh, the elements are *el-* 'much, many'[60] and *ri* < *rigi-* 'king; kingly, royal?' as indeed in Riuallaun, Riuallon. Given occurrence of the latter in earlier, genealogically-claimed, Brycheiniog royal ancestors (Rigeneu, grandson of Brachan, *ri* plus *ceneu* 'whelp'; and Brachan's grandfather, the Teuderic of *De Situ Brecheniauc*, OW Tutri (<Touto-rigi, or the like)), one wonders if this supports a suggestion that Elri was not just an intimate but a blood-relation of the two men.

In all, he included his name four times, the second forwards and second backwards readings being rather more tortuous. Both certainly exist even if, given the previous two, it is unclear (to me) why they were added. Elri has **four** letters, and adds to 40 (E5 L10 R16 I9 = 40). The second forwards reading begins in word no.**4** and uses most of **four** words, *Ioruert Ruallaunque sepulcris iudicii*.

In sindone muti Ioru	17
E rt rua **L** launque sepulc **R** is iud **I**	27
cii adventum spectant in pace tremendum	34
	78

Intervals are 5, 13 and 5; the key number twice, and centrally the 13 representing twelve words (Sons, Disciples) around one central Cross (Jacob, Christ). The first extreme-ratio validation is of letters before the 27-letter span (17) to the span itself (27), giving $17{:}27 \rightarrow 44$, calculated and quite correct ($\cdot382$ of 44 is $16{\cdot}8 = 17$). The second is of the span itself to all the unused letters, 17 plus $34 = 51$; because $27{:}51 \rightarrow 78$, divided by three, gives $9{:}17 \rightarrow 26$ from the set $1.8.9.17.26.43.69\ldots$.

The final (backwards) reading, of perverse ingenuity, is of interest because its mechanism would have been perceived, and was probably imitated, a century and more later by Iago of Llanddewi-brefi in his 12-word memorial for his son, *350 Idnert* of 806. It begins by demonstrating that one of the inscribed names, Ioruert's, is also there in precession-and-interval format. **Ioruert** and **I(n sindone** ...) both start with 'I'. When we notice **I** nsind **O** nemutiio **R** ... with intervals of 5 and 8, we could suspect an interval-sequence from the first Fibonacci number set running $1.2.3.5.8.13.21.34.55...$, and **I** nsind **O** nemutiio **R** uertruallaunq **U** ..., intervals 5.8.13 for **IORU**..., confirms this. The next interval, 21, must take us to an **E**; it does so (**U** esepulcris(+)iudiciiadv **E**) if the central Cross is counted as one 'letter' (graph). Strictly the last two intervals should be 34 and 55, necessitating a run-on, i.e. starting again at the text's beginning.

However, what we find is intervals of 19 and 18 instead: **E** ntumspectantinpacet **R** emendum/In sindone mu **T** (=(**IORU**)**ERT**) – and the pattern might be formulated as 'intervals, Fibonacci series, 5.8.13.21; drop two – 19.18'. Ioruert, 7 letters, has six intervals. Elri, 4 letters, has only three, half that number. Using the reversed passage previously indicated by *retrorsum*, we do find 'Elri', but as follows:

E uqnua **L** laurtreu **R** oiitumenodn **I** = (**ELRI**)

In this, the pattern itself seems to be halved; for 5.8.13.21 we use only 5 and 8, and then 'drop two' from the expected 13 to get 11. The span of the reading is 4 plus ($5 + 8 + 11 =$) 24, perfect 28. ('Perfect' numbers – the first four are 6, 28, 496 and 8128, known to Greek mathematicians – are equal to the sum of all possible divisors including 1 but excluding the number itself; $1 + 2 + 4 + 7 + 14 = 28$, in several inscriptions associated with the Divinity.) Bizarre though this final device is, the demonstrable existence of the author's name four times in his own composition confirms these readings and the extraordinary lengths to which he went. For Elri as a 7th-century mathematician, note that between them the readings show use of (Fibonacci) sets 1.2.3.5.8, 1.4.5.9.14, 1.8.9.17.26 and the widely used (non-Fibonacci) convention 5.7.12.19.31.50, as well as the ability to find the right extreme section of 44.

It has been a guess, not an inference, that Elri was a priest – a guess prompted by his displayed knowledge of the Bible, and by doubts that any layman would go so far as to place even members of his family among the Disciples and in the tomb alongside Christ. A few Insular memorials do describe their subjects as *presbiter* or *sacerdos*. For authors, the Caldey Island slab (ECMW no.301), with its 8th-century dedication for perhaps a royal burial-structure commissioned by Catuocon (Cadwgan) king of Dyfed,[61] reveals mainly by acrostics that it was composed by Unbo and that he was *abbas, Iesu nomine*, presumably of a still-functioning monastery on Ynys Byr. If Elri was a cleric, a further guess would be that one exhibiting what looks like intimacy with the Brycheiniog royalty should have been of bishop's rank, a court bishop whose diocese was loosely the kingdom.

In fact, Elri tells us this. We are back to *sepulcris*; quarry for anagrams and readings, the one word of twelve that seems both forced and parenthetical ('Silent in the shroud Ioruert and Ruallaun (in the graves) await in peace the dreadful coming of the Judgement'). Recall that the key numbers are **five** and **six**, that Elri's name has **four** letters, and that both labelled images, OT and NT, used a square of 36 letters. We see now that words **five** and **six**, SEPULCRIS IUDICII, between them have 16 (square of **four**) letters.

First, there is a validated split reading:

s / **E P** ulcr **I S** iudi **C** / ii = **EPISC(opus)** 'bishop'

in which the abbreviated title[62] has five letters, in order, but with intervals of (twice four =) 8 letters and in a span of 13 letters. This rests on the first Fibonacci number set, 1.2.3.5.8.13.21.34, and can be regarded as properly validated in the usual manner.

Second, all sixteen letters will produce a letter square:

which shows marginal reference to the greater 36-letter square; upper corners S_{17} U_{19} = 36, first three letters S_{17} E_5 P_{14} = 36. It can be seen that 'Christ is at the heart of this' because the four central letters are **C** h **R I** s t **U** s, in that order. One might also find that columns

1 and 3 add to 53 and 58 respectively, their total being 111; and that the word *episcopus* in full, 5.14.9.17.3.13.14.19.17, yields the same figure.

Third, the final touch comes from the fact that anybody who writes out a letter square will automatically glance down at it for acrostics, *more Romano*. Here, we read column four. It offers the telestich **U I D I** (*vidi* = 'I've seen (it)!'). Yes, indeed; and Elri intended you to see that he was *episc(opus)* and composed his text with sacerdotal authority. It would be anachronistic to depict a 7th-century Welsh bishop like a modern Catholic prelate with wide girdle and low-slung pectoral cross, but it is almost as if line 3 of the inscription as a visible display, its midriff as it were, shows something on those lines.

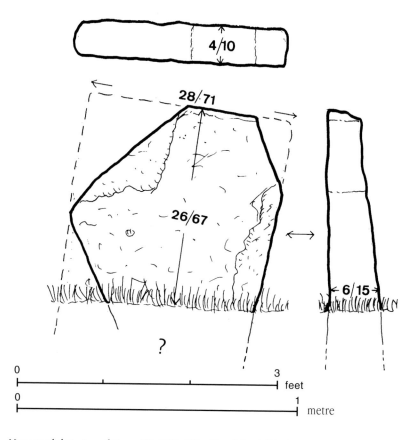

Fig. 7   *Measured drawing of Stone 'A', 1998 (26 x 28 x 6 ins / 67 x 71 x 15 cms).*

The Archaeology of the Tomb

There will be a reasonable supposition that the two upright slabs of the same local rock as the inscribed stone, visible today in the Llanllywenfel churchyard with the western slab some four feet from the external NE corner of the church (Fig.9), somehow represent the items reported in 1699; '…a stone on end [the inscribed slab] in Lhan Lhywenvel Churchyard at the east end. It had another stone eight feet off opposite to it'. Allowing 'feet' to imply one shoe in front of the other, less than a full 96 inches, the present interval between faces is much the same at 93 inches (Fig.10). The crucial, lost, record is precisely what took place in the late 1930s but, if these are genuinely the remains of a post-Roman funerary monument, we could suspect that when the inscribed slab was moved into the church a smaller slab, conveniently at hand, was propped up in its socket to mark the stance. If so, stone 'A' in Fig.9 has been in situ since 1699 and the smaller stone 'B' is the 20th-century replacement; perhaps in origin a remnant of a long-side slab. 'A', which is deeply set (and not quite upright) – Fig.7 – seems wide enough to have been a (western) end-piece.

Insofar as one can find guidance in the memorial itself we might envisage a container in which two corpses, extended inhumations, lay close together below some textile (*in sindone*) but whose deposition was essentially dual (*sepulcris*); or in other words a large cist-grave, east-west internal length at least six feet, burials on or not far below the ground-surface, and most of the tomb visible and accessible, component slabs being sufficiently sunk into the ground to ensure stability and rigidity. In such a scheme the inscribed stone would probably have formed the eastern end, inscription facing outwards, and the overall external width is indicated by that of the stone because the small barred-terminal crosses cut on its thicker edge would have to be visible (Fig.8).

Insular memorials with a text disposed around a central cross are exceptional[63] and in this case yet another function for the stone may be indicated – the equivalent of an altar frontal-panel, within the 'central Cross' category.[64] Did Elri, in his momentary capacity as David to Ruallaun-as-Saul and Ioruert-as-Ionathan, think of a passage from the ending of II Samuel (24, 25), *et aedificavit ibi David altare Domini*? In that sense the above-ground tomb was a species of altar, with frontal panel on a short-end instead of long-side face, and the tomb itself

Fig. 8   *The slab, its face, and edge with small crosses*
         (drawn by Carl Thorpe, 1994)

conceived as (in Braun's classification) a *Kastenaltar*, its hollow interior holding not corporeal relics but entire skeletons.[65] What **is** of significance (shown in Fig.8) is the carving of two (three?) small crosses on the slab's edge, at the height convenient for anybody kneeling in prayer before the 'frontal' to touch them; reminiscent perhaps of the small slate frontal-panel from the Isle of Man[66] with its 8th–9th-century wheel cross, on and around which successive kneeling pilgrims scratched their names, tiny crosses and other motifs.

The reconstructed plan offered here, Fig.10, takes into account that large slabs of the local rock, certainly of the size indicated, can be found in the vicinity; there is an ancient quarry on the Garth ridge opposite Llanllywenfel church. Beyond that, and without an exploratory excavation, we are into guessing. My own guess is that the tomb, if a large four-sided and above-ground monument, was not necessarily lidded but may have been filled to the top with loose stones, an adequate protection for the burials (Fig.11). Not all that much is actually known about 'special graves' of the period, though one possible parallel exists in the Beacon Hill enclosed cemetery on the island of Lundy – a rather larger (externally, some seven by 11 feet) rectangular construction of granite uprights, the interior filled with a considerable cairn of smaller granite stones that covered a central cist-grave burial of normal dimensions.[67] The compound of a mound grave with an Insular version of a *cella memoriae*, as seen on Lundy in the 6th century, may have been repeated here in the seventh.

As for the site, Llanllywenfel churchyard occupies an area of a good acre (or more), parts of whose periphery follow a curve especially on the south. It has the superficial character of a *llan*, Old Welsh *lann*, a noun best rendered as 'Christian locality' but with the rider 'enclosed or physically defined for burial, site of a church and in some cases a monastic establishment'. When it began is again a question that might or might not be resolved by excavation. The ringed crosses on the reverse of the inscribed slab (Fig.12) may imply a primary use as a grave-cover, or a grave-marker, *circa* 550–600; it is, however, not impossible that Ruallaun and Ioruert, battle casualties, were summarily interred here below the slab (marked with these instant crosses) and subsequently translated to a proper tomb, the slab being re-used and inscribed. Presence of a burial of such a social, and it would seem prominently Christian, importance in any cemetery-enclosure would tend here as elsewhere to attract further burials of the faithful, a proximity ensuring some kind of participation in prayers said for the souls of the royal father and son. Llanllywenfel's virtual lack of early history means that we know nothing of the place in late pre-Norman times. Was there a church here before AD 1000? Some continuity of emphasis on the place as a burial-ground is implied by a partial ring of yews,

Fig. 9   *The two standing stones in the churchyard, 94 ins apart. View looking W, at NE external angle of church; nearer, stone 'B' (1939 replacement for inscribed slab?), in background, stone 'A' (in situ?), the slight rubble slope in which they stand is visible. Inset Sketch plan.*

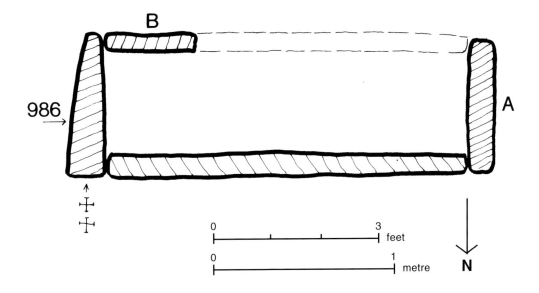

986

B

A

0 ———————————— 3
      feet

0 ———————————— 1
      metre

N

Fig. 10 *Reconstructed ground-plan of the tomb (1998)*

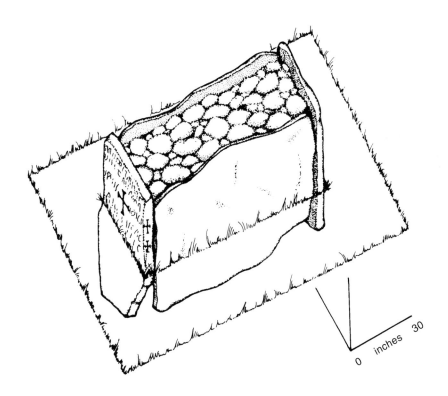

0   inches   30

Fig. 11 *How the tomb may have appeared. An isometric reconstruction.*
(Drawn by Carl Thorpe, 1994)

seemingly of pre-Reformation age, planted inside the enclosure-bank; elsewhere in Wales[68] this is a good indicator of a site's prominence. On the other hand the presence of a relatively sparse population, in ancient times as now, must be suggested by the observation that the interior of Llanllywenfel churchyard is not noticeably raised above the exterior, something that happens (through continuous soil-displacement in grave-digging) in more populous parishes.

Many questions remain (and many possible answers remain elusive). One can dissect the combined OT and NT use of the 36-letter square. Exploitations listed above cover (as a minimum) 34 words and names and eight numerical totals. The average use of each letter is 5·2 times; vowels (6·2.) slightly more than consonants (4). Letter **O**, the first in line 2, is used no less than eight times, the **A** in line 4 and **U** below it each seven times. Much of this would have been planned, written down and annotated, in the construction but some uses probably occurred to Elri as fortunate coincidences in an early stage. 'The mind is a computer' may sound trite but here, and in several other inscriptions, the implicit mental balancing-act, juggling together words, names, allusions, LaN totals, symbolic numbers, part-anagrams, takes us a very long way indeed past any (obsolete) idea of someone who knew a little Latin hacking out clumsy letters on the face of a convenient stone.

Fig. 12 *Reverse of stone*

Summary and Conclusions

Two men whose names are spelled out for us died at or near Llanllywenfel a long time ago. A third man, who intended his name to be revealed, wrote an epitaph for their out-of-the-ordinary tomb. Why?

The first, essential, realisation is that the memorial is more than words to accompany the double burial. In every conceivable way, down to its physical reproduction of an altar-frontal, it is a Christian statement, and as intricate as it is pious. A modern archbishop, even one inured to the instant popular canonisation of persons who could hardly be described as devout when alive, would be astonished at its tone, at the idea that worldly mortals (royal or not) could be ranked with the Disciples and then depicted as within the very Tomb of Christ. And there is no suggestion that Ioruert and Ruallaun were clerics; unlike *350 Idnert*, whose father showed him participating in the Crucifixion, and who in all probability was both a priest and the intended successor as abbot. Nor (one supposes) was such posthumous elevation affected by any previous life. If Ruallaun and Ioruert, as leaders of their people, shared in whatever communal shortcomings could have been believed to bring Divine retribution, as a political catastrophe, down upon the tribes of Brycheiniog, apparently death had squared the books.

The whole exercise of what amounts to a kind of 'archaeology of the intellect' unravelling, through analysis, the stratified features of Elri's composition provides a rare glimpse of a Church-centred literary culture in early Wales. We know that it was not confined to any single kingdom and that comparable epitaphs occur in Anglesey and Gwynedd. Without our having this memorial, and now the means to understand it, one could physically excavate – massively, for years – the entire church-site and churchyard at Llanllywenfel; recover the usual ecclesiastical debris, even skeletal material capable of yielding a C14 date-estimate; but, at the end, remain in total ignorance of the real driving force behind whatever past activities could be reconstructed. This one stone, *986 Ioruert*, symbolises a vanished culture among the British who (in one light) had not ceased to be citizens of a Roman empire that may have vanished, but whose educational system and uniquely significant written and spoken language had been preserved – deliberately – as a bastion against aliens, heathens, who had overrun much of the land.

In composing the inscription the prime purpose was to accord an inflated Biblical and Christian ambience to the dead. Silent and at peace, enshrouded, they may in life have suffered as did the Children of Israel but now their souls await in sure and certain hope the Judgement. All the verbal and numerical symbols spell this out. Secondarily the stone is an announcement that the memorial has been constructed by number and ratio, after the manner of God's own Creation and the teachings of His Word. Each stage (beginning with immediate display), each device, leads on to further proclamations of Number as a Divine attribute. And perhaps a third purpose was to reassure any readers conversant with Biblical style that an epitaph had been created in a manner befitting two men who were of princely rank as well as baptised Christians – whose prominence called for such extravagant comparison. Nor is it unfair to suggest that, finally, all we have seen must (then, as now) provoke a certain admiration; for the literary competence, the ingenuity and the confident piety of the self-proclaimed author, bishop Elri.

Notes

1   *Atlas Brycheiniog* (Llandysul 1960) contains (p.60) a view of a building, the photograph credited to an 'Onfel Thomas'.

2   William Plomer, ed., *Kilvert's Diary 1870–1879*, 3 vols. (new edn., 1960), ii.362–3; this was in August and 'the old tombstones stood knee-deep in the long coarse grass'.

3   Rupert H. Morris, ed., *Parochialia, being a summary of answers to 'Parochial Queries' ... issued by Edward Lhwyd*, 3 pts. (Cambrian Archaeol. Assoc., Cardiff 1910), ii.94 with drawing.

4   Christopher J. Evans, *Breconshire* (Cambridge 1920), 97, 163.

5   M.L. Dawson, brief note, *Arch. Cambr.*, 79 (1924), 413.

6   A lady aged 96, occasional visitor to the church in her youth, remembers it standing outside; two people in their 70s, who would have been children then, can only recall it as within the church. For some decades, use of this church was eclipsed by worship at a modern church at Garth.

7   See, e.g., P.C. Bartrum, *Early Welsh Genealogical Tracts* (Cardiff 1966 = EWGT), Index (of personal names, 168 ff.) under 'Iorwerth' and 'Rhiwallon' (modernised spellings); or Wendy Davies, *The Llandaff Charters* (Aberystwyth 1979), index at 183–4.

8   Matthew 27.59; Mark 14.51.

9   Hence the new word 'sindonology' for its study, and journal *Sindon*.

10 All inscriptions noticed here are cited by numbers, relevant names and/or locations, from Macalister's CIIC as the fullest catalogue (numbered 1 to 1076); some in Wales also with their ECMW numbers.

11 ECMW, 1, n.3; a balanced assessment of his work has been provided by Mark Rednap, 'On Broken Letters Scarce Remembered; Nash-Williams and the Early Christian Monuments of Wales', pp.391–427 in: Joyce Hill & Mary Swan, eds., *The Community, The Family and the Saint* (Brepols, Turnhout 1998).

12 A cornerstone inscription, *970 Catamanus*, dated to c.625, is arguably more likely to be c.660; *Christian Celts,* 163.

13 This is examined at length in my *Christian Celts: Messages and Images* (Stroud 1998), chap 3.

14 Royal Commission on Ancient and Historical Monuments in Wales, *Brecknock: Hill-forts and Roman remains (1986),* 174–6.

15 The area-name is from (Archaic OW) Brachan, with suffix, British and Gaulish *+(i)āco-* 'land, estate, territory (of)', the actual forms showing vowel-affection.

16 Bartrum, EWGT 45.

17 EWGT 10.

18 The full apparatus from several genealogies was examined by David Dumville, 'Late-Seventh or Eighth-Century Evidence for the British Transmission of Pelagius', *Cambridge Medieval Celtic Stud.*, 10 (1985), 39–52, at 50–51.

19 In the Tudor and modern administrative county of Brecknock, the Hundred of Builth forms a north-western appendage.

20 Listed in Howlett, *Celtic Latin Tradition*, 391; one must add Issiu, author of the 7th-century *970 Catamanus* (*Christian Celts*, 167).

21 See my *And Shall These Mute Stones Speak?* (Cardiff 1944), chap. 9, a preliminary statement only.

22 DEB, preface, 10 (transl. M. Winterbottom) '...when they strayed from the right track the Lord did not spare a people that was peculiarly his own among nations, a royal stock, a holy race, to whom he had said "Israel is my first-born son" ' (this, of the British).

23 Her name is from Marcella, close friend of St Jerome's, a pious Roman matron who turned her mansion into a private monastery.

24 1033 (Towyn, Merioneths.), *c*.700 or later, is in Old Welsh throughout; Rachel Bromwich, ed., *The Beginnings of Welsh Poetry. Studies by Sir Ifor Williams* (Cardiff 1980), chap. III.

25 In his *Cambro-Latin Compositions* (Dublin 1998), at 22–3.

26 Fusion of two syllables (ru-a) into one, by coalescence of adjacent vowels without forming a recognised diphthong.

27 For illustrations, see David Howlett's *The Celtic Latin Tradition of Biblical Style* (Dublin 1995), 1–6, and (Jerome's treatment of John 1.1–5) his *British Books in Biblical Style* (Dublin 1997), 79 ff.

28 This bizarre memorial for a re-burial – which is far from what it might seem – is analysed in *Christian Celts*, chap. 7. For the chiasmus, which is Catamanus REX / SAPIENTISIMUS – OPINATISIMUS / omnium REGUM, see Howlett, *Cambro-Latin Compositions*, at 21.

29 ECMW (entry for no. 62), at 77. This is irrelevant; the Kells text of the Four Gospels is by no means pure Vulgate and an Old Latin version was certainly used.

30 He cites Diehl's *Inscriptiones Latinae Christianae Veteres* (ILCV), vol. iii, nos. 3863, 3866–7, etc. Curiously there seems no trace of the phrase in the Spanish corpus with its rich collection of early metrical epitaphs; D. José Vives, *Inscripciones cristianas de la España romana y visigoda* (Barcelona 1943.)

31 *Language and History in Early Britain* (Edinburgh 1953 = LHEB), at 293–6 (and, as R(I)UALLAUN, 386, 456). A more recent view of this is P-Y. Lambert, 'Welsh Caswallawn; the fate of British *au', pp. 202–15 in: Alfred Bammesberger & Alfred Wollmann, eds., *Britain 400–600: Language and History* (Heidelberg, 1990). For the element *uellauno-* see D. Ellis Evans, *Gaulish Personal Names* (Oxford, 1967), at 272–77.

32 LHEB, 294 n. 1, letter of 30 Nov 1950; I cannot quite understand the reasons given.

33 In CIIC ii (published 1949), at 138; Macalister had retired from Dublin to Cambridge during the war and was by now both elderly (b. 1870) and reputedly in poor health.

34 And, earlier, inscriptional usage (from Roman period), particularly on the Continent; in Britain, it appears on *391 Senacus*, *392 Veracius* (NW Wales) and *516 Viventius* (SW Scotland), all *c*.500 and of Gaulish character (see my *Christian Celts*). Superscript abbreviation bars were not, however, adopted for Insular memorials.

35 *Christian Celts*, 176, fig. 72, gives a chronological diagram.

36 Full acrostics have remained popular since Roman times; see Lewis Carroll's poetry. Vives, *Inscripciones* (n.30), gives two nice instances among metrical epitaphs – 281, for abbot Hildemund, 15 lines, acrostic ILDEMUDI ABBATIS, telestich XRISTE MEMOR ESTO, and 282, for an 8th-century bishop Ascaric, 9 lines, acrostic TUSERHEDO (place), telestich ASCARICUS.

37 This is explained further in *Christian Celts* ('Interlude').

38 The pioneer account remains D'Arcy Wentworth Thompson's; his *Growth and Form*, 2nd.edn, (Cambridge 1942), especially chap.xiv. It is updated with a concise mathematical explanation by Ian Stewart, *Nature's Numbers* (1995), chap.9.

39 In 350, they coincide at IACO / BI, showing that the name, though with NT latinisation Iaco-bus, was really 'Iaco' (= Iago).

40 *De Excidio Britonum* (ed. transl. Michael Winterbottom, *Gildas. The Ruin of Britain and other works*, Chichester 1978), preface, sect.7.

41 'The world's wonder – the grave of Arthur', stanza 44 in the Stanzas of the Graves, Englynion y Beddau, from the Black Book of Carmarthen; A.O.H. Jarman, *Llyfr Du Caerfyrddin* (Cardiff 1982), at 41 (line 135).

42 These improbable but well-known ages at death were carried over into Insular hagiography; Patrick, like Moses, lived to 120, and in Rhigyfarch's 11th-century life of St David we learn that he (chap.58) *senium centum quadraginta septem admodum annis complevit* 'fulfilled an old age up to 147 years'.

43 The second e represents the diphthong /ai/ (as in 'mine'): possibly because at this time, in Brycheiniog, graph -ei- was used in the name of Brachan's son and successor Rein, but for a disyllable /re:in/ (as in 'stay-in'). By the 10th century, *Brecheiniauc* is found.

44 *Christian Celts*, fig.2, 49-letter square; the Cross, her name, ground below and possibly her memorial-pillar.

45 *Christian Celts*, fig.8, 64-letter square; the ground, shaft of central Cross with IESUS acrostic, subsidiary cross-shaft.

46 'The Llanddewi-brefi "Idnert" Stone', *Peritia*, 10 (1996), 136–83. This has a preliminary note, 177–8, on *986 Ioruert*.

47 John Wilkinson, *Egeria's Travels to the Holy Land* (rev.edn., Warminster 1981); id., *Jerusalem Pilgrims before the Crusades* (Warminster 1977); E.D. Hunt, *Holy Land Pilgrimage in the Later Roman Empire AD 312–460* (Oxford 1982). In *Vita (Prima) Sancti Samsonis*, the core of which is a 7th-century writing, learned Irishmen on their way home from Rome call at Piro's island, Caldey (cap.xxxvii) – real or not, the episode typifies the ready dissemination of news and ideas westwards from the Mediterranean.

48 Denis Meehan, ed. transl., *Adamnan's De Locis Sanctis* (= *Scriptores Latini Hiberniae*, III, Dublin 1958) – the plans, in the 9th-cent. Vienna Codex, almost certainly reproduce the originals of *c*.683–6.

49 North-topmost is a medieval and modern convention; in the Classical and patristic world, east could be topmost – see passim in O.A.W. Dilke, *Greek and Roman Maps* (1985); Evelyn Edson, *Mapping Time and Space* (1997), e.g. at 16, 'oriented with east at the top ... true of most European maps until the sixteenth century'.

50 See Wilkinson's writings, n.47 above; this can be inferred from details of the church(es) subsequently built over the Sepulchre. For the most recent discussion see now Martin Biddle, *The Tomb of Christ* (Stroud, 1999).

51 DLS, ii.6–14, iii.1–3, pp.44–7 in Meehan's edition (n.48).

52 These are A, the Northumbrian Codex Amiatinus at Florence, 8th cent., and Cavensis, at Cava, Spain, 9th cent., siglum C. A contains OT and NT, C the OT and most of the NT.

53 I have examined this at length in 'Christian Latin Inscriptions from Cornwall in Biblical Style', *Journ. Roy. Institution Cornwall*, n.s.ii, vol.ii. pt.4 (1997), 42–65.

54 So Kenneth Jackson, LHEB 329 n.1; name otherwise unrecorded.

55 From John 21.11 (the miraculous draught of 153 fishes). This occurs in a good many inscriptions. The number 153 is the triangular from 17; Adam, as God's creation, adds up as a name to $1.4.1.11 = 17$.

56 See *Christian Celts*, 50ff.

57 Illustrated in *Christian Celts*, fig.73.

58 In the Penzance Market Cross inscription,1051, set out in 'Christian Latin Inscriptions from Cornwall...', 60.

59 *Celtic Latin Tradition*, 394 (list).

60 This is seen in Eltut(us) (St. Illtud), many names in the Book of Llandaff (Elcon, Elcu, Elgnou, Elhearn, etc.), and in the original name of 'St Teilo', Eliud.

61 *Christian Celts*, 169 ff., full analysis.

62 An unconnected Spanish parallel is Vives (*Inscripciones*), 264, memorial for three bishops (one of whom, Sefronius, died in 550); HIC SUNT SEPULCRA SANCTORUM SACERDO(tum) ID. NIGRINUS EPISC. SEFRONIUS EPISC. CAONIUS EPISC.

63 A small stone found at Peebles (not in CIIC; see *Proc. Soc. Antiq. Scotland*, 101 (1968–69), 127–9 and pl.9) has NE ITANO / SACER DOS around a barred-terminal cross (Neitano sacerdos (?) 'Of-Neitan, bishop'; late 7th or early 8th century).

64 See my *The Early Christian Archaeology of North Britain* (Oxford 1971), chap.6 ('The Altar') for this classification.

65 Joseph Braun, *Der Christliche Altar*, 2 vols. (Munich 1924).

66 CIIC ii, 1068, from keeill in Maughold; about seven different graffiti (names, tiny crosses, little pictures).

67 Probably 6th century, opened (for an enshrinement) in the 7th; described with plans, in *Mute Stones*, chap.10.

68 In Brecon, notably at Llandyfaelog-fach; other instances listed in Vaughan Cornish, *The Churchyard Yew and Immortality* (1946).